My All for Him

Basilea Schlink

Australia: Evangelical Sisterhood of Mary
P.O.B. 430, Camden NSW 2570

Canada: Evangelical Sisterhood of Mary
R.R.1, Millet, Alberta, T0C 1Z0

Germany: Evangelical Sisterhood of Mary
P.O.B. 13 01 29, 64241 Darmstadt

UK: Evangelical Sisterhood of Mary
Radlett, Herts. WD7 8DE

USA: Evangelical Sisterhood of Mary
P.O.B. 30022, Phoenix, AZ 85046-0022

www.kanaan.org

My All for Him

Basilea Schlink

Evangelical Sisterhood of Mary
Darmstadt, Germany

"Should someone be unable to comprehend
some of these truths or expressions,
may he retain at least that which he can recognize
as beneficial and seek to practice it.
With time everything else will become clear to him.
If he cannot appreciate such matters,
he should leave them to those who do
and be wary of blaspheming against things
he does not understand."

—Gerhard Tersteegen
(1697–1769)

What these pages contain are reflections on "first love," bridal love for Jesus, springing from what I myself have experienced in loving Him. I can and must bear witness to the truth of this verse: "Whom have I in heaven but you? And there is none upon earth that I desire besides you" (Psalm 73:25 NKJV). Lord, You are everything!

—Basilea Schlink

Contents

"Only one thing is needed."

Luke 10:42 NIV

I

Of Prime Importance

Supremely important today, as possibly never before, is "first love" for Jesus. Only when we have this love will we be able to bear the hard times that lie ahead, hard times such as the world has not yet known. More Christians have been martyred in the last one hundred years than in the previous centuries put together. We live in an age of great apostasy and widespread deception. Whose faith is strong enough to stand up under intense trial? Who can endure?—Only those who have this "first love" (Revelation 2:4 NKJV), the hallmark of the early Christians. Reports tell of the passionate love for Jesus with which they faced martyrdom; it was, in fact, their first love for Him that compelled them to embrace suffering for His sake.

As we will see, first love is a force to be reckoned with. Its power is greater than the power of suffering, which can have a debilitating and depressing effect on us, making us cowardly and despairing, rendering us ineffective. We need first love in order to persevere. Only one power is stronger than the power of suffering: the divine life contained in love. God is Love.

Whenever He pours out His divine life into human hearts, people begin to love Him intimately and fervently. And nothing in this world—not even the greatest sufferings or horrors, not even martyrdom itself—can quench this divine life, which is immortal, beyond the power of death.

First love—a most precious gift! First love—the one thing that is needed. First love—for which we should pray more than anything else. From Scripture we may infer another name for first love—and that is "bridal love." We read, for example, of Jesus alluding to Himself as the Bridegroom (Matthew 9:15). Then, too, Scripture refers to the marriage supper of the Lamb and to the bride of the Lamb (Revelation 19:7–9). Since the chosen ones of the Lord are collectively called the bride, it follows that individually each possesses bridal love.

From what the Bible says, it is evident that the love between a bridegroom and a bride in a human relationship is but a shadow of the love between the heavenly Bridegroom and His bride. All human love pales in comparison with this first love, this strong, exclusive love for Jesus. Yet there is a similarity. Bridal love for Jesus is undivided like the love of a bride, who has given her heart to her bridegroom and has eyes only for him. In the same way we are to love our heavenly Bridegroom with an undivided heart.

Above all, first love, or bridal love, is of prime importance today in view of Jesus' second coming. When Jesus returns, it will be both as King and as Bridegroom. As Bridegroom He will be coming only for those aflame with bridal love for Him, those whose very love has led them to prepare for their Bridegroom and for the marriage supper of the Lamb.

Bridal love, which we so much need, is not an impossible

goal. Jesus, who first loved us, has planted the seed of this love within our hearts. "We love, because he first loved us" (1 John 4:19). A gift from Him, it is a reflection of His own love and His innermost being. So strong, so pure, so fervent is this love that its potential is unlimited. This love can achieve far more than all natural abilities and strengths, for it is the greatest force in heaven and on earth, possessing the greatest authority because it comes from the heart of Jesus. It was Jesus' love that constrained Him to suffer for the redemption of the world. Bridal love, that reflection of His own love, now gives us the grace to suffer and to sacrifice. Bridal love can impart such strength to us, because it makes us one with the Lord of heaven and earth, the Almighty.

One day, in eternity, we will discover—if we have not already done so—nothing is to be so desired in our life of faith as first love, bridal love for Jesus. It was for this love that we were created and redeemed. This love alone can make us genuinely happy, bringing lasting joy. It is the key to true discipleship. Jesus is waiting for us to love Him with first love, bridal love—for He Himself is the Bridegroom.

*"The kingdom of heaven is like a merchant in search of
fine pearls, who, on finding one pearl of great value,
went and sold all that he had and bought it."*

Matthew 13:45–46

2

First Love—The Great Discovery

For a long time I could not find the key, the answer to my questions: What is true discipleship? What does Jesus want? On the one hand, He calls us to an uncompromising discipleship: to give up everything, to lose our lives. He calls us to leave father and mother. On the other hand, we are to honor father and mother. The Bible also says that the whole creation is the work of God's hands. Since human intelligence and skills are part of that whole creation, should not those aspects of human civilization and culture that are "true, noble, right, pure, lovely, and honorable" (Philippians 4:8 TEV) be held in high esteem? But if we give up everything and live a life of uncompromising discipleship, we become ascetic escapists, rejecting everything God has given. Surely that cannot be right. So what is the answer?

Many voices reached my ears. Leaders from a variety of

Christian traditions tried to convince me that theirs was the only way. One view was that as the body of Christ we should dissociate ourselves from our contemporaries, virtually leaving the perishing to perish. In addition, we were not to concern ourselves with events of national significance. Discouraged from exploring the worlds of art, music, and literature, we were not even to enjoy nature. We were to live in one realm only—the Word of God and the fellowship of believers.

For a while I went along with this, but the reality proved disappointing. Those who subscribed to this view tended to be joyless and lacking in thanksgiving for the heavenly Father's good gifts. Gratitude for the revelation of His awesome greatness in nature was somehow missing. Furthermore, I often found such people narrow-minded and rigid, lacking love for others. At the same time they were very self-righteous, convinced that they had a monopoly of the truth.

Then I heard a very different view, and this, too, I explored. Here were people who were more open, loving, natural, and relaxed. I discovered more of the love and warmth of Jesus in their lives and personalities than I had found in the others. These people did not insist that they alone were the body of Christ. Actually, they did not speak very much at all about their conversion and seemed to be quite at home in the world. Yet this very point made me uneasy. Often they had so conformed to the world that they appeared to have lost sight of Scripture's warnings: "Do not love the world" (1 John 2:15); "Do not be conformed to this world" (Romans 12:2); "Do not be mismated with unbelievers" (2 Corinthians 6:14). They seemed to have forgotten that the Bible calls us as Christians to follow Jesus and go the way of the cross, dying to self and doing without.

Still I wondered, *What does God want? What is His way?* At all costs I wanted to walk in the way of the Lord. After following first the one path for several years and then the other, I still did not feel that I had found His way. But eventually He did answer my plea to lead me "in paths of righteousness for his name's sake" (Psalm 23:3) that one day I might reach the goal of heavenly glory. First, though, He had to show me the truth about myself before He could show me the right way. He had to bring me to the point of spiritual bankruptcy so that I would weep over my sin and see myself for the sinner I was. It was at a time when I had difficulty in getting on with someone who made life extremely hard for me. Resentful and bitter, I could see no way out. We seemed to be hopelessly at odds. I knew this was not right. Yet I was helpless in the situation, unable to resolve it, not knowing how to overcome.

Then the Lord showed me that I was to blame. Had I been loving and merciful toward this woman, she would have been won over. The Lord convicted me of my sin, giving me tears of repentance. And this experience drove me into the arms of Jesus, because Jesus and the penitent sinner belong together. Jesus began to reveal Himself to me in His love. It was no longer a matter of any particular teaching—Jesus Himself was the answer. My intellectual questions began to fade into the background. All I wanted was to love Him who had forgiven my sins, redeemed me, and loved me so dearly. He was now the great love of my life.

To me He had become the "fairest of the sons of men" (Psalm 45:2). The jewel of my heart, the joy of all joys, He was dearer to me than anyone or anything else. With Paul Gerhardt, I could raise my voice in song:

God is the greatest, the dearest and noblest,
Faithful and worthy, unchanging and true,
Best of all treasures, delight of my heart.

He is indeed the dearest of all—He of whom the psalmist writes, "You give them drink from your river of delights" (Psalm 36:8 NIV). Having drunk from this river, I came to love Him more and more.

My love for Him helped me find the answer to my questions. I had found the key—love for Jesus, first love, bridal love. Love became my teacher. I saw that following Jesus had nothing to do with asceticism; I saw that it did not mean renouncing and forsaking the things of this world just for the sake of it. Suddenly I was struck by the significance of the phrase used by Jesus when calling someone to uncompromising discipleship: "for My sake"—"for My name's sake." In other words, we are called to tread this path of uncompromising discipleship out of love for Him. Walking in His steps, we draw very near to the One we love. And this is what true bridal love is all about: being as close as possible to the beloved.

Having shown me that uncompromising discipleship is a free-will decision springing from love, He further revealed that love is the key to Christian freedom. Being the very essence of love, would Jesus not have relaxed at times with His disciples, enjoying God's good gifts? And did He not draw their attention to the beauty of nature—"Consider the lilies of the field . . . even Solomon in all his glory was not arrayed like one of these" (Matthew 6:28–29)? So I, too, was able to enjoy nature—not apart from Him, but with Him, being joined to Him in love.

Now the gifts of the Creator were no longer remote from

me, nor were they to be avoided lest they divert me from true discipleship. Rather, they were tokens of the Father's love. I could enjoy them in the right spirit because they inspired me with thanksgiving and an even greater love for God. I could take pleasure in the beauty of art and music, for instance, seeing the glory of God reflected in them. I was no longer in danger of getting into bondage or being sidetracked from my commitment to Jesus. I could make use of the things of the world insofar as they deepened my love and commitment to Jesus, inspired me with thanksgiving to the Father, or increased the effectiveness of my ministry.

Now everything took on a different appearance. Previously, when I had been trying to lead an ascetic life, I scarcely dared to travel, but now I felt free to do so. Now the motivation was different. In later years, in order to give the Creator glory, I made "praise trips" to scenic spots where praise plaques with a Scripture or song verse would be set up as a pointer to God, inspiring others to offer Him love, praise, and thanksgiving. Similarly, I was blessed when I saw pictures of the marvels of creation or pictures of the beautiful locations in various countries where God had met with me in a special way. Previously, too, I scarcely dared to admire religious art. But now, when I saw pictures of Jesus, I was filled with greater love and thanksgiving. And all this, in turn, had an impact on my ministry, enabling me to glorify Him more.

No longer did I feel cut off from my fellow countrymen, aware only of belonging to the body of Christ. Now that I shared in the concerns of God's fatherly heart, I loved my people and all other peoples, because each originates in the Creator's heart, reflecting something of His love and glory. Now I felt pain when my nation turned from God and rejected His commandments, knowing how this grieved the Father's heart. According to Scripture, although Israel had a special place in God's heart, He was concerned at the prospect of having to destroy pagan Nineveh (Jonah 4:11). And in the light of impending judgment, I came to feel deep concern for my people.

All my questions had been answered. More than that, now I was free. In the past I had feared being trapped either in a life that was too narrow and legalistic or in a life that too readily conformed to the world, neither of which seemed to be true discipleship. Now I had entered the freedom of a child of God, because love bound me to Him completely. Now I belonged unreservedly to the One who is the center of the universe and from whom comes all that is good and noble on earth. In the fellowship of His love I could share in everything that is His— the earth and the whole universe. Though broadened, my love always remained firmly anchored in Him, the focal point of the universe.

Just as I had been unhappy and torn with inner conflict before I found this answer, so I was happy and at peace afterward. Joy had come into my life, because I had found the One who loves me and whom I was privileged to love above all else, with all my strength and being. And for many years now I have gone through life with Jesus as the Bridegroom of my soul. I could never find enough ways to tell Jesus how much I love Him and to praise Him in song as the loveliest and purest of all, majestic and noble, the joy of my heart, the One who brings true fulfillment to my life.

3

The Precious Secret of Bridal Love for Jesus

There is a love that outshines all other loves—a love of unimaginable beauty, strength, and fervency, celebrated by the writer of the Song of Songs. It is the love of Jesus for a bridal soul and the love of that soul for Him. How inexpressibly wonderful that such love exists and that Jesus loves us so dearly!

We can understand Him coming to us as Savior, because sinful humanity needs a Savior; understandably, we will want to thank Him for saving us. We know, too, that Jesus came to us as the One with power to heal our infirmities of body and soul. We can also understand His revealing Himself to us as King of Kings, the Lord of the hosts of heaven, a matchless sovereign clothed with majesty and divine power, at whose command demons flee and wind and waves are stilled. Down through the ages, succeeding generations have expressed their gratitude, adoration, and praise to Jesus, their Savior, Healer, Lord, and King.

What we will never understand is that Jesus wants to come to us sinners not only as King, Lord, Savior, and Healer, but also as Bridegroom. Incredibly, the Lord wants to enter into a love-covenant with sinners like ourselves, just as He did with His chosen people Israel, when He declared, "I will betroth you to me for ever" (Hosea 2:19)—"Your Maker is your husband" (Isaiah 54:5). Jesus pledges Himself to the bride of the Lamb. In forming a covenant of love with her, He forms a covenant of love with each individual soul, male and female, who is a part of that whole company, His bride, the bride of the Lamb.

From Jesus' words "Whoever loves Me . . ." and "Do you love Me?" we sense how much He yearns for us to love Him. But it is a special kind of love He seeks. It is the love that is reflected in the relationship between an earthly bride and her bridegroom. An exclusive love. A love that tolerates no rivals. A love that gives the beloved, the bridegroom, first place. As the heavenly Bridegroom, Jesus lays claim to such first love. Because He loves us so dearly, He longs to have the whole of us. Jesus gave Himself unreservedly for us. Now He yearns for us to give ourselves completely to Him, with all that we are and have, so that He can truly be our first love. To offer Jesus anything less than this first love is of little value to Him. So long as our love for Him is a divided love, so long as family, possessions, and the like mean more to us than He does, then so long will He consider our love not to be genuine. Indeed, Jesus will not enter into a covenant of love with one whose love is divided, for a covenant of this nature requires a full, mutual love. How Jesus yearns for our love. But because our love is so precious to Him, He waits for our wholehearted commitment to undivided love.

True love for Jesus will always choose Him when faced with an alternative. If, for example, Jesus calls someone to the mission field, then for Jesus' sake he leaves his native land. This could involve separation from loved ones, including children, and possibly even—albeit temporarily—his wife. Love for one's country and family has to take second place. Jesus can only be our true love, our first love, if our love for Him takes priority and, when having to choose between Jesus or people and things, we choose Him.

Jesus has every right to make such a claim upon our love, because He has no equal. No one is so glorious, so majestic, and yet so winsome as Jesus. His love is so compelling, so tender and intimate, so fervent and strong that no human love could ever compare with it. No one loves us so faithfully, loves us as if we were the only one. No one is so caring. No one is available so exclusively for us as Jesus. Jesus knows what He can give with His love. He knows how deeply happy He can make a person. That is why He has the right, a thousand times more than any bridegroom on earth, to say, "Give Me everything—your whole love. Make Me your first love, for which you would leave all else behind, just as an earthly bride would give up her home and native land, indeed all her desires."

Can we hear Jesus pleading with us, asking for our love? He wants to have the whole of us, no area of our life being withheld from Him. He will tolerate no rival love. Loving us fervently, He is grieved when we do not return His love wholeheartedly, loving Him with all that we are and have. His love for us is so powerful that He yearns to receive our deepest love. Yet for a true bride of Jesus, nothing could be a greater source of joy than devoting herself completely to Him, giving her love, her all, to the One who loves her so ardently. She regards it as sheer grace to be His very own.

God's very own—blessed words! God has claimed me for Himself. And He loves me so deeply that He is not satisfied until I commit myself completely and unreservedly to Him. Only the one who loves Jesus in this way can understand Him in His essential being and taste His deep and intimate love.

Do you remember the story of the rich young ruler (Matthew 19:16–22)? Jesus loved him, and deep down inside this rich young man longed to love God. Jesus saw his desire for eternal life and, ultimately, for a life of loving union with God. God is both life and love. Whoever receives eternal—or divine—life, also receives God's love. Everyone, including those trapped in sin and materialism, longs deep down inside for happiness and a truly fulfilling life, but these can only be found in loving God.

Jesus showed the rich young man the way. Attaining riches in heaven, eternal life, requires giving up something else, in fact, everything. This is inevitable, for eternal, divine life means wholehearted loving. Giving my whole love to Jesus means letting go of all else that I love.

The rich young man went away sad. And to this day—as I know for myself—Christians are often somewhat rigid and joyless. We have missed out on joy, all because we lack that vital, ardent love-relationship with Jesus, which is supreme happiness. So long as we do not give Jesus our first love, we will not have this relationship. Perhaps we are afraid of falling into false asceticism or legalism, but usually the real reason is that we are in bondage to material possessions or to our prestige, career, loved ones, and so on. We have not given Jesus our undivided love.

When I gave Jesus everything—not just in prayer but in practice, surrendering to Him all I held dear, loved ones as well as intellectual and cultural pursuits—I entered a love-relationship with Him. He revealed His love to me as Bridegroom and let me taste the fullness of life.

Jesus' message to the rich young ruler could be summed up like this: *Sell, give up what you have, follow Me, commit yourself to Me and My way. Out of love, give Me your life and everything that makes it rich and worthwhile for you. Give it to Me— not from any ascetic or other motive, but as an act of love. And I will give you the eternal, divine, overflowing life of love with its far greater riches; this life will make you happy beyond all imagining.*

Jesus can ask this of us, because He is "the Life." Those who commit themselves to Him are joined to the very source of life and love.

Whoever follows Jesus in this way receives divine life. Such has been my experience. For years I had lived on "cheap grace," unresponsive to His call to uncompromising discipleship as binding for my life. Then came the time when His love overwhelmed me. And then as His disciple I consciously chose to walk in His ways. In day-to-day life I tried to live out the Sermon on the Mount, choosing lowliness and poverty, turning the other cheek, not insisting on my rights, keeping silent when wronged, and in time of hardship, as during the war and post-war period, sharing even the last of my possessions, in keeping with Jesus' word, "Give, and it will be given to you" (Luke 6:38).

From then on I knew for myself that whoever follows Jesus is really joined to the One who is eternal life, to the spring of love that flows unendingly. I discovered that this spring of love is poured out most into the hearts of those who know they are sinners. Not until I had begun to take Jesus' call to discipleship seriously was I faced with the true, divine standards for my life. Time and again I sinned against them, but my repeated failures actually drove me into the arms of Jesus, impelled me to claim His redeeming blood, and reopened the fountain of His love.

Just how much Jesus cares about us loving Him is evident from His visit to the home of Simon, the Pharisee (Luke 7). He prized the visible tokens of love from the sinful woman who kissed His feet and anointed them with ointment, perhaps her most valuable possession. This was love directed personally to Jesus. This was ministering to the Lord Himself rather than to others. Our service to others in the name of the Lord has its place and should flow out of our love for Jesus. But Jesus values even more our personal devotion, treasuring a love centered on Him, a love lavishing gifts on Him, and for which no sacrifice is too great, a love that has eyes only for Him.

> The true bride says to Christ: "I do not want what You have to give. It is You I want. You are not more dear to me when I am doing well, nor less dear when I am doing poorly."
>
> —Martin Luther (1483–1546)

In Gethsemane Jesus waited with a yearning heart for His disciples to watch with Him in His hour of need, just to be with Him, showing that they cared. But He sought and waited in vain for this evidence of their love. In Bethany, just before His

Passion began, He had also looked for love. And there He did find someone who entered into His pain, appreciating how heavy His heart was because of His imminent suffering and death. It was Mary. Love revealed to Mary of Bethany that His soul was in anguish, and she did what she could for Him. Her concern was Jesus Himself. That was why she did not give her money to the poor, a fact for which she was rebuked by the disciples. Instead she lavished her jar of costly ointment on Jesus (John 12:1–8). Sensing His deep pain, she longed to comfort and refresh Him.

I will never forget the time when the realization gripped me: Since Jesus is the same today as long ago, His heart grieves still today. And so He is waiting for us to bring Him joy, to refresh Him, and indeed—as Scripture says—to be comforters to Him (Psalm 69:20). Ever since then my primary concern has been Jesus Himself rather than my service for Him. I continued to carry out what He had called me to do, but now there was a shift of emphasis. Now I was concerned with ministering unto Jesus. A fire was kindled in my heart as I saw the importance of worship. It grieved me for His sake that He received so little love in words and songs of adoration. Since then worship has never been absent from my prayer life. Although I am a pronounced active and social type, from that time on I felt a compelling desire to spend every free minute in my room to commune with Jesus in prayer. I sensed that He was waiting. Does not a bridegroom always wait for those private moments with his bride when they can open their hearts to each other?

Jesus yearns for fellowship with us and to hear words of love from our lips. He wants to draw near to us. He wants to speak to us in our hearts and nurture a loving relationship with us. Only in times of quiet, away from the hustle and bustle of daily life, with nothing and no one to distract us, can Jesus give us His love more fully and more intimately. If we long to know the presence of Jesus and to enter into bridal love for Jesus, let us be faithful in our quiet times, keeping them holy for Him.

Jesus is waiting for our love. Our sacrifices are important to God, so, too, our obedience to His commandments. Jesus commended the rich young ruler for keeping the commandments. Yet this obedience on its own could not bring him eternal, divine life. Only love could. However, making sacrifices and keeping the commandments are not necessarily inspired by love. Jesus knows this, and being Himself the very essence of vibrant life and love, He wants to share these treasures with us. To Him, our love, stemming from the divine life He has given us, is the only acceptable response to His love for us. Then love, in turn, will prompt us to keep His commandments, for love respects the wishes of the beloved, and His commandments are His personal requests to us. Love will compel us to make Him many gifts and sacrifices, though in a completely different spirit now, because the motivation is different.

There is something wonderful about this love for Jesus. All bridal souls carry this love for Jesus as the most blessed secret and treasure in their hearts. Even if they do not speak of it, everyone having anything to do with them senses something of this precious secret. There is a joy and a radiance about them, the radiance of love, for they love Him who is the fairest of the sons of men. They love Him who shines like the sun in all the heavens, the entire universe. They love Him who reigns in majesty and glory. They love Him who loves them with a tenderness no human heart could possibly give. They love Him who has revealed Himself to them as their Bridegroom.

Love is a dynamic force. It radiates happiness and great joy. The heavenly Bridegroom is the Lord of joy, anointed with the oil of gladness (Psalm 45:7). His bride shares in this joy. She belongs to Him who shines like the sun in His love, joy, and light. Because she is joined to Him, her personality reflects something of His joy and radiance. Nothing in the world can bring such immeasurable happiness as love. An earthly bride's delight in her bridegroom is but a pale shadow of the true, eternal joy felt by the bride of the Lamb for her heavenly Bridegroom. There is no greater, happier, higher, richer love than bridal love for Jesus.

> Before the world had e'en begun
> You loved me, Father, in Your Son,
> The holy Sole-Begotten.
> To Christ betrothed, to be His bride
> And ever with Him to abide,
> I sing for joy and gladness.
> Trials, troubles cannot grieve me,
> Nor dismay me,
> For in heaven
> Everlasting life awaits me.
> —Philipp Nicolai (1556–1608)

"The only bliss which we possess on earth is loving God and knowing that He loves us."

Curé d'Ars
1786–1859

4

Love—The Highest Calling

Love—most blissful of words! God is Love; He radiates love; and love is what makes heaven "heaven." Love is the word that rings through heaven as a joyful sound. The redeemed in heaven love one another, because they all love Jesus, the heavenly Bridegroom and King, who is one with God the Father and with the Holy Spirit.

We, too, may love Him and, in loving Him, share in the nature of the triune God, which can be summed up in one word: love. Through love the world was created. Through suffering love it was redeemed. Through love it will be transformed into a new earth, along with a new heaven. Love shines out of every flower God made. Love prompted God to make creation so beautiful for our enjoyment. Love fills the Father's heart and moves Him to give His good gifts so generously—all that His children need in this life. Love inspired Him to create heaven as a place of never-ending bliss and happiness, where those who love Him will dwell in the mansions of the Most High.

Love constrained Jesus to suffer and to die in order to open the gates of heaven for us. Love prompted Him to go before us to the Father and prepare a place for us that we might always be near Him, who is Love eternal. In His love He wants to lead us on to the supreme happiness for which we were created: loving union with God.

Love, bridal love! Who can comprehend its secret? It is too deep, too high, too wide for us to ever fully fathom. For bridal love speaks of the heart of Jesus, the heavenly Bridegroom, beating with compassion for His bride, a sinful human being. With tender love He surrounds her, caring for her supportively, conscious of her slightest concern, ever at her side to help and protect. He gives her a new dignity, enhancing her beauty.

Who can compare with the heavenly Bridegroom, who is Love eternal? He did not keep this love to Himself; rather, He created and called us to love Him, who alone can give us the joy of true love and deepest fulfillment. What a privilege! We may drink from His river of delights. We may love Him who will never disappoint or fail us. We may love Him, the Royal Lord, to whom we sinners are joined as His bride. We may love Him, the Ruler of the universe, with whom we will someday rule all worlds.

We may love Him who is the fairest of all because He bears the marks of His wounds as the sign of supreme love. We may love Him as the Man of Sorrows, who poured out His love in immeasurable suffering for our redemption. No price was too high. In Gethsemane His soul nearly died as He suffered intense anguish, His sweat as blood, His appearance changed beyond recognition for sheer terror and agony. When scourged, His whole body was covered with wounds. Words cannot describe the depth of His pain when mocked and despised. Arrows of hate pierced His heart. Was He not the Son of God, whom all the angels served and through whom we were created? Now He was no better than a worm, fit only to be trampled upon—and all this even though He had only lived to bring love, help, healing, and the message of the kingdom of heaven. Such love defies comprehension.

We may love Him who bore His cross quietly and patiently. He carried all our burdens, taking them to the cross, to which He was nailed in indescribable agony. Tortured to death, He gave His life on that cross so that His blood, flowing down upon this dark, sinful, satanic earth, would redeem those who claim in faith the power of His blood. We may love Him who as victorious Lord rose from the grave, demonstrating the triumph of love over death and hell, and who now shares His resurrection life with those who love Him.

The One we are privileged to love is the sum total of all love, the One most worthy of love in heaven and on earth. Unbelievably, He loves us. We were created and saved that we might love Him. Blessed are those who hear Him ask, "Do you love Me?" and who respond, "Lord, You know everything. You know that I love You."

"If anyone thirsts, let him come to me and drink."

John 7:37 NKJV

5

The Royal Offer

There is One who walks through the streets, knocking at the doors. He has something to offer. What is it? It is His love. Everyone He meets He stops to ask, "Will you take what I have to offer—My love? You are looking for something to make you happy, aren't you? You would give good money for it, devote time and energy to searching for it. But now I am offering you My love. In it you will find everything you are looking for and everything that could make you happy. Take My word for it and accept My offer."

"What must I do to receive it?" you ask. He replies, "Make room so that My love can flow in. My gift of love has no equal. But there is this one condition: that you make room for it. I cannot make this gift to a heart that is already filled. I am looking for an empty heart. Empty your heart of everything filling it, and you will find the most valuable gift, the most wonderful gift in all the world: a love relationship between you and Me—the deepest, closest, purest, holiest, and strongest possible. Surrender all else, and you will find it!"

Those who accept in faith this royal offer of love, opening their hearts to Jesus and dedicating themselves to Him as His bride, will come to know Him as their one and only love. What Jesus offers surpasses anything that this world can offer.

Jesus as Love everlasting
Descended from on high
To show to sinful beings
The way of love divine.

Jesus as Love everlasting
Enkindled many souls
To dedicate their everything
For love of Him alone.

Jesus with love still is seeking
For hearts aglow with love,
Their lives and longings yielding
To Him who's from above.

Once more the Savior is knocking
At every heart and door.
Oh, can't you hear Him pleading,
"Accept Me as your Lord"?

"I will betroth you to me forever;
I will betroth you to me in righteousness
and in justice,
in steadfast love, and in mercy.
I will betroth you to me in faithfulness;
and you shall know the Lord."

Hosea 2:19–20

6

Jesus—A True Bridegroom

Jesus is everything a bridegroom should be. As is evident from various Scriptures, He longs to have a bride. The love of His bride means so much to Him that He is always looking to see whether she will rise and come to Him, whether she really longs for Him alone.

Being a Bridegroom, Jesus wants to give you His love, but He also wants to receive your love in return. Being a Bridegroom, Jesus will not tolerate a divided love. He wants the whole of you. He watches over you with a holy jealousy. He is anxious that you do not devote more time, energy, and love to people and to things than to Him. When you do that, He is grieved, His hurt being a measure of His love for you.

As a true Bridegroom, Jesus will not force you to love Him. He only asks, "Will you give Me your love?" Nothing less than your love will satisfy Him. The fact that you believe in Him, obey Him, and have received His forgiveness for your sins—all this is insufficient for Him. He is not just the One who heals you. He is not just your Redeemer, who delivers you from the chains of sin. He wants to be your heavenly Bridegroom and to love you with a deep, tender, intimate love. Now He is waiting for you to give Him your love. Love by its very nature both gives and receives.

As our Bridegroom, Jesus is wounded when we embrace a life of poverty and self-renunciation, taking up self-chosen crosses—simply for ascetic reasons. Certainly He wants us to follow Him on the way of the cross. But His heart is grieved and offended if it is not love that motivates us. We are not supposed to follow the way of the cross for our own sake and the sake of our sanctification, but rather—as He said while on earth—for His sake. For His sake we are challenged to lose what makes life worth living for us, even parting with our homes and loved ones, should He call us to do so. Love for Him should be our sole motivation for leading a life marked by poverty, obedience, lowliness, humility, and disgrace. Only love-inspired dedication is pleasing and acceptable to Him. All else is too little. Anything else is more likely to wound Him, because it is hypocrisy: While outwardly we seem to be walking in His footsteps, it is really only for our own sakes. Hence His challenge: "Do you really love Me? Give Me your love, and you will give Me everything!"

Jesus, the Bridegroom, is the Man of Sorrows, who knows pain and grief to this present day. He is looking for a bride who will share the innermost concerns of His heart. His heart is filled not only with love but also with suffering—today as long ago.

He is looking for a bride who will live up to her calling, whose heart will beat with His, who will share His burdens. He is looking for a bride who is not totally absorbed in her personal sorrows but will identify with His, entering into the fellowship of His sufferings (Philippians 3:10). She alone is a true bride of Jesus who has a heart for His concerns: the troubles of humanity, the difficulties within the church worldwide, and everything hindering the advance of His kingdom.

For Him, the bride is the soul who suffers with Him and who is prepared to do everything to alleviate His pain. In prayer she asks her Bridegroom what grieves Him and how she may comfort Him. Then, knowing what will comfort His heart, she does all she can to change those things that are troubling Him. She strives that He will receive love and honor, wherever He is denied this. She yearns for reverence for God to be stirred up where there is none, longing intensely for a move of repentance where His laws and commandments are disregarded. With consuming zeal and passionate ardor she self-sacrificially loves, suffers, labors, and spends herself to win for Him souls who will accept His lordship and begin to love Him. Not until her Bridegroom is comforted will she be satisfied.

Jesus is in every way a Bridegroom. This is why He is not satisfied with mere slavish obedience. He desires our heart, our total dedication. As our Bridegroom He asks, "How much am I worth to you? How much are you ready to sacrifice for Me? For love of Me can you give Me your loved ones—children, parents, friends? Can you give Me your home and country if I ask for these? Are you willing to comfort Me in this way? Will you go anywhere I call you in order to save souls? Can you sacrifice your prestige, your strength, your longing to be loved, your deepest secret wishes—for love of Me?"

Jesus is a Bridegroom in the truest sense of the word. He waits for His bride, because the kind of love He seeks cannot be forced. He knocks gently on the door, waiting to see whether the door will open and His bride will let Him in (Song of Songs 5:2). He is grieved when His bride is overabsorbed in her work and earthly matters. In her daily tasks she may be quick, active, full of initiative, but Jesus' eyes follow her sadly if she is always rushing about doing things while becoming estranged from Him.

Jesus is a Bridegroom with every fiber of His being. His burning concern is to give His beloved new dignity for the very reason that she is His bride. He yearns for her to be adorned with many virtues and to reflect His divine loveliness. He works with loving care to shape her into a vessel worthy of Him. He trains and disciplines her along paths of chastening, so as to raise her to His side. He looks ahead to the day when full beauty will be hers. He loves her too much to permit her any blemishes or wrinkles, for she is His bride. Full of pride and joy, He gazes at her in His love as though she were already perfect. He, by the power of His blood, can change her bit by bit until she does reflect Him (Romans 8:29; 2 Corinthians 3:18).

As the heavenly Bridegroom, it is Jesus' nature to stand protectively at the side of His bride. He is intent upon defending her from all who may wish to harm her. He strives on her behalf. Being a bride means you are no longer alone; it means having a loving companion who feels completely responsible for you and who is always available for you, even ready to risk his life for you. As the heavenly Bridegroom, Jesus feels honor bound to help His bride in all circumstances, in every hardship and impossible situation. He will never leave her on her own. True to His nature, He waits longingly for the day when His bride will be united with Him forever in the heavenly glory. With infinite love He waits for her to come.

There's one alone my soul adores,
For whom alone I care.
Besides Him there is no one else.
None can with Him compare.

O pure and spotless Lamb of God
And Bridegroom of my soul,
Oh, make me ever one with You,
Who triumphed o'er the foe.

I praise Your wounds, O Lamb of God
Who died to save us all.
Your holy, precious outpoured blood
Brings healing to my soul.

There's one alone my soul adores,
My Savior, Jesus Christ.
None other bore such pain and woe
As He who for me died.

*"I stand at the door and knock. If anyone hears my voice
and opens the door, I will come in and eat with him, and
he with me."*

Revelation 3:20 NIV

7

Knocking at the Door of Our Hearts

As our heavenly Bridegroom, Jesus is standing at the door of our hearts and knocking. Are we not filled with awe to know that the ceaseless adoration of cherubim and seraphim, indeed of all of the heavenly host, cannot satisfy His deepest longings? Are we not amazed that He desires something more—our love? Incredible though it may seem, Jesus humbles Himself to draw near to us. He stands knocking at the door of our hearts, pleading, "Give Me your love." Do we realize how often He repeats this request in His longing for us? It is in responding to His love that the treasure of bridal love becomes ours.

> O love of God most holy,
> You came from God's own heart,
> A Beggar meek and lowly,
> To every human heart.

Beyond man's understanding
Is such humility,
God pleading that we love Him!
What will our answer be?

Alas, alas, too often
Your pleading is in vain.
Your love beyond all measure
Is treated with disdain.
To see You suffer anguish
The angels weep above,
But who else heeds Your pleading,
O Beggar, for our love?

From soul to soul You wander.
You knock at every door,
Desiring deepest union
With us for evermore.
Your very heart You offer
As loving Lord of all,
But we, preferring others,
Ignore Your fervent call.

O Pilgrim, how much longer
Along earth's dusty roads
You're still obliged to wander
In search of loving souls?
Far more than royal power,
The glory and the crown,
A loving heart You offer,
Which surely none would scorn.

Accept our love, O Bridegroom.
To You we give our heart

To quench the ceaseless longing
Within Your loving heart.
Oh, make in us Your dwelling,
That love divine and true
May keep us ever burning
And one, dear Lord, with You.

*"No love can make us perfectly happy
other than love for God.
And no faithfulness can give perfect bliss
other than that binding us to Christ."*

Søren Kierkegaard
1813–1855

8

Believe His Offer of Love

If I wish to attain bridal love, I must believe that Jesus is standing at the door of my heart, waiting to be invited in because my love means so much to Him. Jesus is asking you and me the all-important question: "Do you love Me?"

Behind this question lies Jesus' desire to be loved. He asks for our love. It is precious to Him, and what He most desires. This is the question He asked Peter after His resurrection (John 21:15). By implication, it is the question of the risen Lord to all of us who know how He suffered and died for us out of love: "Do you love Me? Will you respond to My love by giving Me yours? Will you give Me your heart, so that there is nothing else in it but Me alone?"

If you cannot grasp the depth of Jesus' desire for our love, then ponder the first commandment, which is to love God above all else: "You shall love the Lord your God with all your heart, and with all your soul, and with all your mind" (Matthew 22:37).

If you still cannot believe it, then hear the outpourings of God's grief in the Old Testament. He would lament that although He was Israel's husband, time and again she forgot Him, her love evaporating like a morning mist in the sun (Hosea 6:4). Great was God's lamentation when Israel repeatedly gave her love to people and to transient things rather than to the One who had covenanted His love to her. Our love must mean a great deal to God; otherwise its being denied Him would not cause Him such deep sorrow of heart.

"I have loved you with an everlasting love" (Jeremiah 31:3). Let us listen to this assurance of God's love, also to be found in Jesus. If only we would believe! For Jesus it is not enough to have saved us and to have set us free from the devil's bondage. He wants to give us more. He wants to enter into a covenant of love with us for time and for eternity. In His love He yearns for us to be united with Him, to be in Him, to share everything with Him.

"When I passed by you again and looked upon you, behold, you were at the age for love; and I spread my skirt over you, and covered your nakedness: yea, I plighted my troth to you and entered into a covenant with you, says the Lord GOD, and you became mine" (Ezekiel 16:8).

Some may still have difficulty believing that Jesus loves us as intimately as a bridegroom loves his bride. Surely their doubts must yield when they consider the promise in God's Word that those who "wait with love" for Jesus to appear will be crowned (2 Timothy 4:8 TEV) and those who overcome will sit with Him upon His throne (Revelation 3:21). Wanting to have someone always at one's side is a sign of love. Jesus loves His bride so dearly that He wants her to share His throne with Him in the heavenly glory. He wants to have her near Him forever.

I remember the time when I was so moved by this realization that I dedicated myself to Jesus as a bride of His. How awesome to think that He wants to do everything with His bride. With her He will one day rule the universe and judge the nations. And it is because of His desire to be forever united with His bride that He will hold a wedding celebration. How could God call heaven's greatest festival a wedding—signifying a union of love—unless Jesus were the Bridegroom, and unless His bride, the bride of the Lamb, consisted of bridal souls with a passionate love for Jesus?

In His love, Jesus longs to be one with us. This is why He stands at the door of our heart, asking for our love. For our part, we must be ready to respond if we want to attain bridal love. This calls for an act of surrender and declaration of love by us, preferably in writing to show that we are serious. In a human relationship love is a two-way matter. It is not enough for a man to tell a woman that he loves her: She has to return this love, committing her life to him—otherwise she is not a bride. Jesus is waiting for the response of our love. Not until we affirm our love will the blissful stream of His love flow into our heart. His love, which is divine life, streams into our heart only insofar as we commit ourselves to Jesus.

My Jesus,
I pledge myself to You,
my loving Savior and Bridegroom

Christ Jesus,
to be Yours wholly and forever.
I renounce evil with all my heart.
Any hold that Satan may have over me is broken.
As of now I am Yours,
my Bridegroom of blood,
who through Your agony in Gethsemane
purchased me to be Your own possession and bride.
You destroyed the gates of hell
and opened the Father's loving heart for me
as You wrestled in prayer
and sweated blood in the Garden.
From this moment on
may my heart and all my love
be wholly devoted to You in gratitude.
For now and evermore
may not my will but Yours be done.
Rule and reign in me.
I grant You authority over me
and promise, with Your support and assistance,
to let the last drop of my blood be shed,
rather than deliberately or knowingly,
inwardly or outwardly,
be unfaithful or disobedient to You.
Behold, I am Yours completely,
sweet Friend of my soul.
I will cleave to You
with the pure love of a bride.
May Your Spirit not depart from me.
May Your agony in Gethsemane
give me the strength to endure.
Yea, Amen! May Your Spirit seal

what I have written in simple words
as Your unworthy possession . . .
    Gerhard Tersteegen
    Maundy Thursday, 1724

Love for Jesus is the commitment that says: "Take my life and everything that makes life worth living for me—people, things, hopes, dreams, all my aspirations. Because I love You, I simply must give You everything." Love holds nothing back. Love wants to give the beloved that which is especially cherished. Anything less is not worthy of the beloved.

What Jesus is asking of us is so simple. All He wants is our love. Can we believe this? He desires of us something so beautiful—not just obedience but fervent love. Nothing can make us happier than loving Him. Human love cannot compare with this bridal love for Jesus. People can disappoint us, and a human love-relationship can quickly cool. But we are privileged to love Him who will never disappoint us and who loves us beyond all telling.

If you wish to have Jesus completely,
give yourself to Him completely.
If you wish to experience the fullness of His love,
love Him unreservedly.

9

Forsake Everything for Him

Although Jesus stands humbly knocking at the door of our hearts, He has lost nothing of His royal dignity. He knows that in offering His love He is offering the greatest blessing for time and for eternity, the greatest gift a person could ever desire or receive. This is why He challenges us to such radical discipleship, saying, "Whoever of you does not renounce all that he has . . ." (Luke 14:33); "He who loves father or mother more than me is not worthy of me" (Matthew 10:37); "If any one . . . does not hate his own father and mother . . . and even his own life, he cannot be my disciple" (Luke 14:26).

When Jesus, speaking with royal dignity, makes such statements, it is essentially as a Lover. He does not utter these words primarily as a Teacher, nor even as the Lord demanding obedience. Rather, He says these words as a Bridegroom. In the "wedding-song psalm," celebrating the love between bride and bridegroom, the psalmist writes, "Hear, O daughter, consider, and incline your ear; forget your people and your father's house; and the king will desire your beauty" (Psalm 45:10–11). The Bridegroom calls the bride to forget everything, to leave all else behind for His sake, so that He can delight in her.

We can almost hear Jesus asking, "Whom do you love most? Me, Jesus? Or yourself, people, and things?" To Jesus, this is the question that matters most. And this is why the words "for My sake . . ." accompany Jesus' challenge to give up everything. The call to part with everything for His sake is understood only by the soul who loves the Lord with bridal love. If a bride truly loves her bridegroom, she is willing to leave home, career, and native land just to be with him. Such demands are annoying, even offensive, to those who do not love with bridal love. Love, however, by its very nature is self-sacrificial, desiring to give all for the beloved.

As a loving Bridegroom, Jesus has every right to ask, "Will you give up everything for Me? Will you seek only My love and approval? Are you willing to give up your dearest and best in order to win the dearest of all—Me—and My love? Am I worth so much to you that you would give up everything for Me? Is My love worth more to you than the love of people? Do you love Me? Do you love Me more than anything else?

"Do you love Me like this?" asks Jesus. "Only then will you come to know My love, unlike those who give Me only a little love and whose hearts are divided. I do not reveal My heart to them. I do not lavish upon them My love and the riches of My love. They will not experience for themselves how I repay one-hundredfold every sacrifice. Wanting the best of both worlds, they will receive nothing. They will be satisfied neither with human love and the things of this world nor with My divine love and My gifts. I am unable to give them the fullness of My blessing. I reveal Myself only to those who genuinely love me. And it is they who will be filled with heavenly joy, even in the midst of suffering, because I, the King of heaven, Love itself, make My dwelling in them."

Have you ever considered the consequences, for this life and the next, when you love Jesus with a divided heart? You miss out on the greatest blessing of all—and, in the world to come, you will not have another chance. Only those who have loved Jesus with the single-minded devotion of a bride will be able to join in the marriage supper of the Lamb, that event of supreme joy celebrating the union of love between Jesus and His bride—the moment all heaven awaits.

The Bridegroom is knocking at your door. If you want to know His love, then surrender your dearest and best in order to win the dearest and best—Jesus. He seeks an undivided heart. Heed His constant plea: "I want all of you." Commit everything to Him. Yield to Him all your thoughts and feelings, emotions, desires, and aspirations. . . . Our love for others is to flow from our love for Jesus, who alone is to be our first love. He lavishes His gifts on those who love Him above all else. Such souls He loves with all the fullness of His love.

Nothing could be greater and more blissful in heaven or on earth than knowing Him and His love. But this doesn't just happen. Rather, it is the reward of those who give Jesus their all. They become more and more Christ-centered, every desire of their heart directed to Him, every impulse of the will merging with His. The bride is gripped with this one longing: "You shall be my one and only love." Jesus does not share His love with anyone whose commitment is halfhearted. When drawn into the orbit of Jesus' love, however, we will want to give up everything for Him. And if we ask Him, and trust Him, then He will make us completely His.

Oh, make me Yours,
Beloved Lord and Savior,
That I may praise You through my life
    forever.
Oh, make me Yours.

Oh, make me Yours.
You are my life and treasure.
My life, my all, to You
    I now surrender.
Oh, make me Yours.

Oh, make me Yours.
You died for me, dear Savior,
And so my heart belongs to You
    forever
In gratitude.

Oh, make me Yours
With all I am and have, Lord,
And all I value, so that I
    may comfort
You with my love.
Oh, make me Yours.

*"Her sins, which are many, are forgiven,
for she loved much."*

Luke 7:47

IO

The Sure and Certain Way

A woman comes to Jesus. Her heart is so burdened by reason of her sin that she falls at Jesus' feet and can only cry. Her heart is filled with sorrow and anguish because of her sin. She is overwhelmed by guilt toward God and others. Yet this is the woman of whom Jesus said, "She loved much." In demonstrating her love for Jesus, she made up for what the Pharisee had neglected in his duties as host. This is why Jesus asked him which of two debtors would have the greater love for a money-lender who cancelled their debts; and the Pharisee himself gave the answer: "I suppose . . . that it would be the one who was forgiven more" (Luke 7:43 TEV). Someone weeping over personal sin, someone who loves much. . . .

Forgiveness of sin is the true source of 'bridal love. This woman's tears and contrition opened the way for her to love, her sins having driven her to Jesus. Her grieving heart helped her to see not only her sin but Jesus Himself. She saw how lovely He is and how worthy of love. The hearts of those who cry over their sins, who seek and receive forgiveness, are opened—and into such hearts Jesus pours His love, which then flows powerfully back to Himself. Just as this woman previously loved the world and her sinful pursuits, so now she was led to abhor these things, to repent of them with tears, and to love Him.

This woman cannot sufficiently express her love for Jesus. She anoints His head and washes His feet. In Eastern countries foot washing was a service of love normally extended to guests arriving after traveling through the hot sand. Jesus' host neglected this courtesy. Yet this woman, moved by love, washed His feet—not with water, which she could easily have drawn at no cost to herself, but with her tears. She poured out her heart in tears of repentance and in gratitude for forgiveness. Every tear flowing from the pangs of contrition was an expression of her love.

From Jesus' words we see how deeply touched He must have been by such a foot washing. He had never known one like this before. It must have refreshed and comforted His heart. If there is joy in heaven over every sinner who repents, how great must be the joy over a sinner who ministers to the Lord with a loving, penitent heart.

Yet this woman does even more. A special, intimate proof of love among human beings is the kiss, and she cannot help but kiss the feet of Jesus. Her heart is gripped by Him who loves her, who has forgiven her, who came to earth to save her from all her sins and make her whole, and who calls her to His side. Possibly she was one of the women who followed Him around the countryside during His time of ministry, later to be at His side in heaven for all eternity.

Jesus was the focus of her love. Her concern was Jesus Himself. She was not primarily interested in His having dealt with her guilt. No, her heart was kindled with personal love for Him. She had to do something for Him. And so she gave Him what His heart most deeply desires: love in response to His boundless love.

This is why Jesus said, "She loved much"—the greatest tribute He can pay. The issue was love for the Lord. Here was a soul who loved Him greatly and whose love, flowing from repentance, led her to do something beautiful for Him. In our lives, too, such love for Jesus can flow only from a heart that grieves over its sins. Daily we sin against God and others, and daily the Lord waits for us to show that we are contrite; through repentance it is possible day by day to minister unto Him with our love.

If our desire is to have and to nurture bridal love, then our urgent prayer must be: "Show me daily what a sinner I am in the sight of God and man. Give me a contrite and broken heart like this woman. Help me daily to weep over my sin so that I humble myself in spirit before You and before those whom I have hurt or wronged. Help me not to shrink from the pain of seeing my sin, acknowledging it, accepting responsibility and any consequences; for in no other way can You grant me the grace of tears that speak of my love for You."

He will answer such a prayer, because His heart longs more than anything for this love born out of repentance. A fountain of love will spring up in our hearts, and Jesus will have in us a bride ministering unto Him with overflowing love.

I come with tears and weeping,
Beloved Jesus mine,
For grieving You with sinning,
O holy Love divine.
My heart cries out, lamenting
The error of my ways,
"Though I am undeserving,
Forgive me in Your grace."

A sinner who was straying
Is now restored to grace,
With tears and laughter mingling,
While singing songs of praise.
To save me from hell's clutches
You went to Calvary.
My thankful heart rejoices,
"From sin You set me free!"

Now I can bring You glory,
Dear Savior, with my life,
In gratitude for mercy
Refresh You with my love.
My failure brought me blessing,
Inspiring praise and love.
My heart is ever singing
The mercies of the Lord.

The grace of repentance not only opens our eyes to see our Savior and makes us fall in love with Him but also prepares us for the fellowship of His sufferings. This can be seen in the life of Peter. We recall his answer to the risen Lord: "You know everything; you know that I love you" (John 21:17). A tremendous statement. In effect, Peter was declaring, "Nothing is hidden from You. All mysteries are known to You. You know what is happening in the whole universe, as well as what is going on in every single heart. And so You know that my heart is consumed with love for You." It may come as a surprise that Peter could make such a declaration so soon after denying Jesus. An admission that he had failed to love his Lord might have been more expected. Yet Peter could not help but speak as he did. From the serious sin of denying Jesus had sprung tears of repentance, tears that clarified his vision, enabling him to see Jesus as He really is: the Man of Sorrows, who with infinite love gazes upon those who pierce Him to the heart, as Peter himself had done.

This experience revolutionized Peter's life. Now his heart, overflowing with love for Jesus, cried out, "I love You. I just have to love You. My heart, my life, all that I am and have, I surrender to You. I am ready to suffer for You, because I love You." And Peter was later to make good his word.

No matter the cost in terms of suffering, true love will never desert the Beloved. Always to be at the side of the Beloved is the mark of overflowing love born out of repentance.

"Where I am, there shall my servant be also."

John 12:26

II

Searching

Whoever has discovered the precious secret of bridal love for Jesus and tasted the joy of finding the Bridegroom of our souls will also discover that it is possible to "lose" Him. Allegorically, this may be seen in the experience of the Shulammite, who wandered through the streets at night seeking the one she loved (Song of Songs 3:2–3), because he was suddenly no longer with her. To those who love the Lord, no grief could be greater, for they would say: "My heavenly Bridegroom is the only one who makes me truly happy. Even if I have everything I've always wanted in this life—but not Him—then I am without the most precious of all. There is only one who satisfies the deepest longing of my soul. Without Him, I drift—lonely, aimless, in darkness, in a spiritual desert—with no one to return to. He was the One who always welcomed me home."

When bowed down with trouble and distress, the bridal soul discovers that only her heavenly Bridegroom brings her relief. Not only is He quick to see what is weighing her down, but He is also strong and carries her burden. She knows beyond all doubt: "If I have lost Him, then there is no one else to whom I can turn, no one else who really understands me in my innermost being. My heavenly Bridegroom is the only one able to help me. He knows and understands me, because He made me. His loving eye penetrates the depths of my being, noticing even the slightest emotion. He knows what stirs my soul, what makes my heart ache, what fills me with yearning. He sees and understands it all, and so He alone can help me."

The bride of Jesus declares, "I must have Him. Having Him, I need no one and nothing else, for He gives my life its ultimate fulfillment. My soul was made for Him. He alone—my Lord and Bridegroom—satisfies my deepest longings. I cannot exist without Him. If I lose Him—through my own fault, because of my indifference, by going my own way—then it is as if my life were extinguished. I no longer have the One who alone can make me happy with His love. My joy is gone. And since it is He alone who can cause such joy in my heart that even suffering fails to get the better of me, then, if I lose Him, I am the unhappiest of beings: defenseless in the face of temptation. My heavenly Bridegroom is no longer there to fight for me and to protect me from the attacks of the Evil One. He could do for me what I in my weakness cannot do. Now I have no one to sustain me when I am weak. What hope is there for me now?"

The bride of Jesus is further aware: "Not only can I not live without Him, but I am spiritually bankrupt when I have lost Him. Without Him I cannot do anything fruitful, anything that would bless others and make them happy."

What should the bride do in her great distress? Like the Shulammite, she should arise and seek Jesus, her heavenly Bridegroom. So long as we are on earth, there will be times when we lose Him, as the Shulammite lost her beloved. We lose Jesus when we fail to commit our will to Him. We lose Him when our thoughts are taken up with people, things, or self—work, prestige, or personal pleasure—rather than with Him. We lose Him when we yield to sinful inclinations instead of bringing them to Him to be cleansed by His precious blood.

No tragedy could be greater than that of losing Him. Without Him we are like chaff blown about in the wind. Without Him we are at the mercy of the powers and principalities threatening us on all sides. That is why we need our Lord Jesus Christ as our loving Bridegroom.

Where do we find Him whom our soul loves? Where can we be sure always to find Him?

There are certain landmarks along His pathway—and there we will find Him. Bridal love means being where the Bridegroom is. Since Jesus does not recognize any other type of love as bridal love, no matter how much we seek Him, we shall never find Him if we do not look in the places where He is to be found.

Jesus lingers at those places where He was to be found during His earthly life. These places have not changed. They are the places of lowliness and humiliation, self-denial, sacrifice, and suffering. Figuratively speaking, we can hurry through all the streets and squares like the Shulammite and still not find Him, simply because we are not looking in the right place. It may be that we are reluctant to go to the place where Jesus is; we may find it disagreeable there. But if a bride tells her bridegroom that she loves him, she proves her love by wanting to be where he is. If his duty lies in some foreign land or in some place or situation she would naturally dislike, she shows her love by following him. She wants to be with him at all costs.

If we look for Jesus where He is, we will have Him as our Bridegroom. He will then share with us His joy, His help, His power, His strength—all the wonderful blessings that are His to give. Our every need will be supplied. However, we cannot keep affirming our love for Jesus, our heavenly Bridegroom, and not want to be with Him. The moment a married woman refuses to accompany her husband when he moves somewhere, she has disrupted the relationship of love. A separation has occurred.

Very quickly it can lead to divorce. What happens on a human level is but an indication of what can take place between us and our heavenly Bridegroom. Divorce occurs the moment we no longer want to be where Jesus is. True bridal love for Jesus can only grow deeper and more intense as we earnestly desire to share His path of lowliness, self-denial, and sacrifice, to go with Him to those places that spell suffering and death to self.

Let us make the testimony of Ruth our own: "Where you go I will go, and where you lodge I will lodge . . . where you die I will die, and there will I be buried" (Ruth 1:16–17).

> Where my Lord goes, there I would go,
> Sharing with Him both joy and woe,
> Close at His side for evermore.
>
> Clasping the hand that's pledged to me
> In love for all eternity,
> I would now follow step by step.
>
> May I have eyes, Lord, only for You,
> Thinking of You in all I do,
> Bringing You joy as a true bride.

Oh, let me share Your lowliness,
Sovereign Lord of the universe,
Laid in a manger long ago.

Help me to heed not pain and loss,
Die to myself, embrace my cross
In body, soul, and spirit too.

May I fulfill each wish of Yours,
Wholly devoted to my Lord
As a true bride, who is all Yours.

"Jesus Christ is the same yesterday and today and forever."

Hebrews 13:8

12

The Man of Sorrows Today

Where do we find Jesus, our heavenly Bridegroom? Where can we find His heart? Two thousand years ago His Passion was the hallmark of His love. Jesus Christ, being the same yesterday, today, and forever, still lives and loves and grieves over the sins of humanity. He also suffers in His followers. Again today He is mocked, rejected, condemned—in them. If we are to find Jesus, we must go to those places where His disciples could have found Him on His way from Gethsemane to Calvary.

The disciples could have found Jesus, becoming one with Him in love, had they watched with Him in Gethsemane. But they fell asleep, failing Him in His hour of need. That is why they lost Him and, in losing Him, were overcome by a sense of hopelessness and despair.

I will find Him whom my soul loves when I am willing to tarry in "Gethsemane," the place where my world collapses and I am in turmoil, crying out in distress, "Where is my God?" I will find Him when my heart bleeds (just as Jesus sweated drops of blood in Gethsemane) and yet I say, "My Father, Your will be done." This means accepting His will even when coming under spiritual attack. For Jesus, Gethsemane was the final preparation for His death on the cross. We, too, can expect to be attacked by the spiritual hosts of wickedness (Ephesians 6). When we endure such inner conflict with our will yielded to God, we are being prepared for our Calvary, where we are crucified with Jesus (Philippians 3:10).

When have we found our Bridegroom? We have found Him when, drawn to His side, we say,

> My Jesus, here will I kneel beside You
> At this rock of Your fear and agony.
> Out of love will I stay with You
> When You lead me through the dark valley.
> I will stay by You.
> I will endure to the end with You . . .*

The disciples could have found Jesus in the Kidron Valley as He was led as a prisoner to the house of the high priest. But they were not with Him there. They had fled. That was why they were plunged into misery and despair. Had they stayed with Jesus, allowing themselves to be bound as He was, then

---

*Text of the plaque in the Gethsemane Grotto in the Garden of Jesus' Sufferings at Kanaan, Darmstadt, Germany. Kanaan is the headquarters of the Evangelical Sisterhood of Mary, an international, interdenominational organization founded in 1947 within the framework of the Evangelical (Protestant) Church in Germany.

they would have experienced His sustaining power, His peace, and a measure of His glory. But they had forsaken Him. They had no peace of soul, only inner torment.

At His arrest Jesus said, "I am he" (John 18:5). In effect, He was saying to the guards, "Take Me, bind Me, lead Me wherever you will. All this is happening with My Father's consent." If we want to find Jesus today and to be with Him, this means being willing to be tied down to a place or job that may not be to our liking. We will have fellowship with Jesus if we are willing to give up our freedom and personal desires instead of hankering after a seemingly easier and more attractive life.

Where is the One whom we love? At what other place can we find Him? The place of judgment. Here again His disciples failed Him, not one of them testifying on His behalf. With their Master taken prisoner and standing trial, they must have been in utter despair, their hopes completely dashed. But the deeper and real reason for their despair was their failure to be at the side of their Lord and heavenly Bridegroom.

Whoever is willing to go with Jesus to the place of judgment will surely find the Bridegroom, for He is still there today. Perhaps we wonder at times why Jesus seems so far away. Yet how simple it is to find Him. Let us take our place beside Him who was falsely accused. The disciples failed to stand at Jesus' side long ago. That was why they were so unhappy and far away from Jesus. And they had only themselves to blame.

If we were at least willing to accept criticism when it is justified, that would be a start. It does not need to be anything big—perhaps just having a mistake or failure in everyday life pointed out by others. We lose the Bridegroom every time we refuse to accept valid criticism. Jesus is to be found at the place where He was accused by the judges. If His bride were to go there, she would be united with Him immediately; and even while judgment was being passed on her, she would have a foretaste of heaven. The first step is to be silent when rebuked. We need to do as Jesus did. Though innocent, He was silent in the face of unjust accusations. As sinful human beings we have all the more reason to remain silent. But if we are too proud to accept even justified reproof, we rupture our bridal relationship with Jesus and align ourselves with Satan, who fell because of his pride and rebellion.

Now we know where we can find Jesus. As He stood before His judges then, so He stands accused today. Millions of false allegations are hurled at Him. When He stood trial long ago, He did not find a single defender among the thousands to whom He had ministered help and healing in sacrificial love. No one forced his way through the crowd to say a word in Jesus' defense. If we really love the Lord, we will not look to human help when wronged or falsely accused. Yet at such times we will be especially close to Jesus.

We will indeed find Jesus at the place of judgment, for this is where He spent the greater part of His Passion. He was dragged before four different judges; and later, even as He hung dying on the cross, false accusations were flung at Him. The place of judgment meant intense suffering for Jesus. But if we do not want to be where our Lord is, we lose Him. Then we need to search for Him until we find Him by coming to repentance, when He can be one with us again.

Yet if we cannot even bear to hear the truth about ourselves and admit our faults, how can we possibly stand with Jesus at the place of scourging or at the place where He was crowned with thorns?

At such places it is not only false accusations that await us; we may also be faced with acute anguish, disgrace, slander, ridicule, loss of reputation . . . But Jesus, our heavenly Bridegroom, is also there. We will find Him at the place where He was crowned with thorns, as at any of the other places marking His Passion. Spiritually uplifting experiences, should Jesus choose to give them, have their place. These, however, do not necessarily bring about union of love with Jesus. Rather it is in suffering ridicule and disgrace that we become one with Jesus in love.

Spiritual blessings, including the gift of bridal love, are ours only when we see ourselves for what we are: sinners in the sight of God and man. Remove this foundation, and we are in danger of fantasizing and becoming hypocrites. We are no longer walking in the way of the Lord. Although we may still claim to belong to Jesus and to be close to Him as a bride, in reality we are far from Him.

But if we go to the place of suffering—which can also be physical, as with pain, weariness, or illness—Jesus is one with us, and love's glory begins to shine. We find Jesus on the way of the cross, when such a heavy burden is laid upon us that we feel we can no longer stand erect. If we feel bowed under the weight of various burdens and the Lord continues to add fresh burdens, then we may know that He is especially near. Yoked to Him, we will receive all that is His to give in the way of love, help, comfort, deepest understanding, sympathy, refreshment, heavenly joy, and blessings.

Then comes the moment when we actually choose the

place of crucifixion, the place that spells death for everything our natural selves cling to. When we are yielded to this death process, allowing our longings to be nailed to the cross through God's leadings and dealings, we will be united with our heavenly Bridegroom. Then we will also bear His marks: the wounds. Jesus was inflicted with wounds along every step of the way. From the beginning of His Passion, He bore the wounds of the soul. Then came the scourging, when His body became a mass of wounds. The wounds intensified and multiplied at the crowning with thorns and the bearing of the cross. Finally, at Calvary, nails pierced His flesh.

There are times in our life when Jesus may call us to share in a particular stage of His sufferings, though our suffering will be on a far smaller scale than His and, in a sense, never undeserved, for we are sinners. Only when we bear wounds willingly, as Jesus did, will He recognize us as His true bride. We should rejoice in the suffering we bear in body, soul, and spirit, for then we are close to the Lord Jesus as His bride. Peace flows into our hearts, and we will share in the victory and glory arising from Jesus' sufferings.

Our love for Jesus and our union with Him will deepen if we are not afraid to seek Him where He is to be found: at the place of suffering. It is there that Jesus waits for His bride. And it is then that we will come to know our heavenly Bridegroom in the fullness of His nature. We will see how much He loves us and cares for us, sustaining us and giving us victory over besetting sins. We will taste the joy He gives even during suffering. In Him we have abundant life. All this will be ours, provided we seek Him where He is to be found.

O Man of Sorrows, I declare
My love for You undying.
No other glory can compare
With that of Yours in suffering.

O Man of Sorrows, in Your pain
Forgiving, ever-loving,
The loveliness of suffering grace
Your countenance reflecting.

O Man of Sorrows, radiant
In anguish and affliction,
My heart inspires with reverence,
A passionate devotion.

For You alone I want to live
With all my heart and being.
Lord, make me true and sensitive,
One with You in Your suffering.

O wound-scarred Lamb, I will exalt
And bless Your name forever,
And never leave You all my days,
For I am Yours, dear Savior.

*"As often as I write the name of Jesus,
a holy tremor passes through me
with the joyful fervency of gratitude
for the assurance that Jesus is mine.
Not until now did I really know
what we have in Him."*

Johann Christoph Blumhardt
1805–1880

13

Jesus—Loveliest of Names

First love, bridal love, is nourished only when put into practice. Think how easily the love of married couples can diminish with the passage of time. It becomes "rusty" if not expressed, if words of love are absent, if a loving attentiveness is missing, if love-gifts are no longer exchanged. Love begins to diminish when one no longer has loving thoughts of the other or no longer pronounces the name of the other in loving tones.

The true bride of Jesus carries a secret in her heart: the name of her Bridegroom. "Your name is like perfume poured out" (Song of Songs 1:3 NIV). It has been my experience that when the name of Jesus resounds in my heart as the name of Him whom I love above all else, when I repeat it again and again, my love for Him is fanned into flame. New songs would flow continually from my heart as I celebrated His name in song. "O the name of Jesus, most glorious name of all, I will sing Your praises."

Incredibly, we may appeal to this name; we have the right to do so. A bride is entitled to use her bridegroom's name. Finding herself in difficulties, she will naturally use his name, so that doors will be opened, obstacles removed. The heavenly Bridegroom rejoices when His bride, filled with pride and joy at having such a Bridegroom, makes frequent use of His name. Whenever I call upon the name of Jesus, I am filled with awe. What a wonderful Bridegroom! What a Prince of Victory! He has fought and won the battle against Satan, trampling him underfoot. My Bridegroom is the risen Lord, who sits at the right hand of God. At the name of Jesus chains of sin are broken, the powers of darkness put to flight.

"This is my beloved," says the bride in the Song of Songs. He is the Almighty. He is the conquering Lord of Lords, the all-powerful Victor. When I call upon the name of Jesus, evil forces yield, and oppression is lifted. I am privileged to call upon the name of Him who loves me and who is devoted to me, as I am to Him. Because He loves me, He wants to help me. Jesus is there to stretch out His powerful hand, to demonstrate His might and glory on my behalf. When I pronounce His name in my heart, something happens. Repeating the name of Jesus or the phrase "Jesus is Victor" during intercession has an impact on souls in bondage. Prayers need not be long to be effective; indeed, in times of testing and distress, long prayers may not be possible. I can only say that when I have trustingly repeated the name of Jesus, peace flooded my heart and help came.

The name of Jesus will sometimes sound like the resonant chiming of bells in the heart of the bride, at other times like the soft music of the lyre. There is so much love and tenderness contained in this name. To carry the name of Jesus in our hearts is a priceless gift, one that can never be taken from us. How precious it has been for me to repeat the name of Jesus in my heart during times of spiritual dryness or when I was ill and prayer did not come easily. Nothing could stop His name from ringing in my heart.

What power lies in pronouncing the name of Jesus! It is the most effective prayer! Yet we should not pronounce this name simply because it makes us happy and brings us peace and help. We should also do so for His sake, sensing how it delights His heart. Saying His name lovingly deepens our relationship of love with Him. A word expressive of our love for Him (and do we not always express love by saying the name of the beloved?) will not go unanswered. As we lovingly utter His name, Jesus answers and offers His love to us. It is the love of His bride that draws Him to her. Jesus said, "He who loves me . . . I will love . . . and we will come to him and make our home with him" (John 14:21–23). The song of our love, expressed in saying His name, is irresistible to Him. He cannot fail to enter a heart that awaits Him, lovingly repeating His name.

It is vital that we put our love for Jesus into action. This happens not only by saying His name in our hearts, or aloud, but also by expressing in words our love and gratitude for His love and for His sufferings. Even when not in the mood, we should still sing Him a song of praise and worship. Our hearts will be kindled anew with love for Him when we sing and declare who Jesus, our Bridegroom, is: the King of Kings, the Lamb reigning in majesty upon the highest throne, the very essence of love, the mighty Prince of Victory, the fairest of the sons of men, the splendor of heaven.

I have found that whenever I ceased to adore Him in word and song, my love-relationship to Him became languid. At such times we run the risk of lapsing from first love, bridal love. There is great power in praising the attributes of our Bridegroom. When we declare who He is, the glory of His nature shines upon us. If previously we were lukewarm or depressed, absorbed with cares, people, or things, we rejoice in Him again. As we praise Him for who He is, His uniqueness will be evident: None can compare with Him. When we see the power of His love, glory, and greatness, everything fades away that might have obscured His love, made Him seem remote, and ended our intimacy with Him.

In uttering the name of Jesus and in worshiping Him for who He is, we nourish bridal love. Our love for Jesus is constantly under attack from Satan, who begrudges us this supreme happiness. Like a roaring lion, he prowls around, trying to find where we are vulnerable. He wants to break into the chamber of the bride's heart so as to disrupt her loving fellowship with Jesus. He has many methods of enticing us with people and the things of this world so that we fall into bondage. When we succumb to temptation, we break the bond of love with Jesus, who will not tolerate a divided heart.

We are called to battle against "the wiles of the devil" (Ephesians 6:11). His enticements will lose their power as we focus on Jesus and proclaim Him in all His glory. Then all that is counterfeit will be seen for what it is in the light of His glory. Those who fail lose the fellowship of love with Jesus. But those who faithfully nourish bridal love, calling upon His name, will reach the heavenly goal—the marriage supper of the Lamb.

Jesus! Name all heaven is singing!
Name with which all heaven is ringing,
Throbbing with exultant joy!
You are 'throned in splendor glorious,
Crowned with crowns of beauty wondrous
More than man can comprehend.

Jesus! Heaven's joy and wonder,
Shining like the sun in splendor!
Jesus! Name most sweet to hear!
Angels, all-adoring name You,
As their sovereign Lord acclaim You,
As their God and Maker own.

Listen to the voices swelling,
One by one are they retelling
Tidings of dear Jesus' name.
Heaven with that sweet name is ringing;
Countless choirs, its glory singing,
Sound the praise of His great love.

Jesus, glorious name resplendent,
Every bliss and joy transcendent
Dwells within Your heart of love.
Heaven kneels in awe adoring,
Whispers softly of the glory
Of Your love and majesty.

"Whatever your task, work heartily, as serving the Lord and not men."

Colossians 3:23

14

For You

We nourish bridal love not only by lovingly pronouncing the name of Jesus but also by doing everything out of love for Him. This lightens the burden, even during difficult, demanding work. No longer dependent on what appeals to us by nature, we find that unpleasant tasks become a source of joy.

> With Jesus the bitter becomes sweet.
> If the bitter has not yet become sweet for us,
> we have not yet entered the fellowship of love with Jesus.

The Lord wonderfully helped me to discover the secret of doing everything out of love for Him. While still a young woman, I began to suffer severely from rheumatism. As traveling lecturer for the Women's Division of the German Student Christian Movement, I traveled extensively and often had to sleep on makeshift beds. Consequently, I had many sleepless nights. I had difficulty accepting this wholeheartedly, and my love-relationship with the Lord was marred. Later, I repented deeply that I had not been ready to bear a few inconveniences and discomforts for love of Him, trusting in His help. I asked the Lord to give me an opportunity to make up for my failure and prove my love for Him. In response He led me into another traveling lectureship, this time for a missionary society. During World War II my job took me to all parts of the country. Again, there was physical discomfort, as I stayed in unheated rooms and traveled on overcrowded trains. Added to this was the danger element in the form of air raids. Being fearful by nature, I can only say that I found this a very difficult ministry.

Then the Lord gave me two simple words that transformed everything: *for You*. This little phrase, an affirmation of bridal love, helped me greatly in all my troubles, even overcoming my fear. Whenever I was reminded, "Here is something I can do or suffer *for You*—for love of You," the things hardest to bear became easy. Everything changed. Saying *for You* also helped me later at work to abide in His presence throughout the day and taught me to do everything in union with Him. Whenever I became overengrossed in my work and tackled it apart from Him (even though it was all work for the kingdom of God), these two words helped me. Like wings they lifted me up to the One I loved. *For You, for You, my Lord Jesus* would ring in my heart.

What infinite power lies hidden in bridal love, for it unites us with the almighty Creator of the universe! If we do everything in union with Him, saying lovingly *for You*, the impact is far greater than anything imaginable. Then everything we do, whether peeling potatoes or routinely operating the same machine day after day, produces great fruit for the kingdom of God, because work done in loving communion with Jesus has lasting value.

Why? Because love is the greatest power of all. Loving

union with Jesus is spiritually dynamic. A person may be ill. Yet if he endures everything for and with Jesus, this union will have far-reaching effects, bearing fruit for eternity. My prayer became: "Let me do everything today with You. May my every thought, word, and deed flow from my union with You. Do not let me be separated from You today. O Holy Spirit, admonish me when I cease to abide in Jesus." I had discovered that our lives can be fruitful only when we do everything in union with Jesus.

Jesus your Bridegroom wants to have fellowship with you. Can you hear Him calling?

> Do everything for Me.
> Give Me your best time.
> Abide in Me all day long.
> Do not think, speak or do
> anything apart from Me.
> Remember that every time
> you tear yourself away from My heart,
> it hurts Me, because we are one.
> Keep your eyes not on your work but on Me.

Say in reply to your heavenly Bridegroom:

> Jesus, You shall be first in my life.
> I want to talk with You and work for You.
> I want to think over everything with You,
> making all my decisions with You.
> Nothing shall be done without You,
> for I do not want to shut You out of my life.
> Bind me tightly to You,
> so that nothing—

no work, no burden, no other interest, no joy—
can separate us during this day.
So may I constantly live in Your holy presence:
for You are here!

May this day be dedicated
To You, Jesus, dearest Lord.
Troubles, cares—whate'er it brings me,
May Your name be praised, adored.

Lamb of God, beloved Bridegroom,
Grant Your grace to me this day,
That I may reflect Your image
In whate'er I do and say.

Help me to endure each trial,
Dearest Jesus, hear my plea.
Even on the hardest pathway
May You, Lord, be seen in me.

May I live to bring You glory
When Your name is so despised,
In all things, whate'er may happen,
Prove myself Your faithful bride.

Every time we dedicate our will to God
in whatever happens to us,
the union of love takes place.
This is an absolute and certain union
and therefore the purest and highest.

15

Committing Our Will

Bridal love for Jesus is nourished and grows when we daily bind ourselves to Him. The dedication of the will leads us into the deepest union of love with Jesus. The true test of bridal love is the willingness to submit wholly to the will of God, even when He frustrates our dearest wishes or we cannot understand what He is doing either in our lives or in the lives of others. To nurture bridal love and to show Jesus that we love Him, we need constantly to practice submitting to His will and wishes.

Often I have been led along paths on which my hopes and desires were shattered. My prayers went unanswered and I could not understand what God was doing. Then the realization struck me: *The time has come for the genuineness of my love to be tested. Even though I cannot understand God now, there is something I can do: I can prove my love for Him by loving His will.* Knowing that His will is always good, always love, because it springs from His loving heart, I began to praise the loving will of God in song: "God's will is goodness, His heart all-loving, His leading always wise and best." This helped me to immerse my will completely in His, so that, despite my pain and inner turmoil, peace came into my heart. My fellowship of love with Jesus was restored. Once again I was one with Him. Gone was the barrier I had raised by resisting, however slightly, the will of God.

By complaining, asking why, or rebelling against God and His actions, we create a barrier. But we need to know: If our unity with the will of God is disrupted, so is our unity of love with Jesus. We have ceased to abide in Him. We have lost our first love. If we are to foster bridal love for Jesus, we must not allow even a hint of rebellion against the will of God. Bridal love is a delicate plant. Without the right soil, it does not grow but withers. And the right soil is unity of our will with His. Do we realize how lovingly Jesus regards this little plant in our hearts? Often He watches us sadly from afar, because we no longer have our eyes on Him. Our unity of will with Him has been broken. Should we not make the most of each day, striving to be fully surrendered to His will? What a unique opportunity to bring joy to our heavenly Bridegroom!

I long to love You,
No longer grieve You,
Spend all my life for You, Jesus, alone,
True comfort bringing,
Souls for You winning,
Those who will follow close in Your steps.

Balsam I'm bringing,
From deep pain springing,
Like precious perfume outpouring for You.
This shall refresh You,
Comfort, uplift You
From pain and suffering sinners inflict.

Love's balsam flowing
Out of my yearning
Only to live to bring joy to Your heart.
Trust when I can't see,
Trust You entirely,
This is like costly ointment to You.

Has this world any
Task that's more worthy,
Task of great glory to serve such a King,
Bring to my Savior
Comfort and pleasure,
Fall at His feet in homage and love?

"We are the temple of the living God."

2 Corinthians 6:16 NIV

16

Christ's Indwelling

God the Lord, who calls Himself the Husband of His chosen people, announces, "The Lord has chosen Zion; he has desired it for his habitation: 'This is my resting place forever; here I will dwell, for I have desired it' " (Psalm 132:13–14). Could anything be more wonderful? This promise is echoed in Jesus' assurance to His bride, the soul that loves Him: "Anyone who loves me will heed what I say; then my Father will love him, and we will come to him and make our dwelling with him" (John 14:23 NEB).

The Lord is looking for a heart in which He would be happy to dwell. These verses from Psalm 132 were displayed in the room where our Girls' Bible Study Groups used to meet in 1944 and 1945 during the revival. I wanted this text before my eyes because it expressed the greatest desire and the most fervent longing of my heart: that the Lord would say to me, too, "Here I will dwell, for I have desired it." To me, nothing could be more wonderful than the Lord saying He wanted to make His dwelling in us.

In John 14 Jesus tells us where He wants to dwell: in the one who loves Him. It is love that draws Jesus to make His dwelling there, and it is love that keeps Him there. This love is not about feelings, but rather depends on the unity of our will with His. The love drawing Jesus to dwell within a human heart is a love unwaveringly committed to Him, even during difficult times. It is a love at one with Him.

"I come to live within you."
Our Lord and Savior Jesus
Says this to every Christian soul.
"Prepare for Me a lodging
With ardent love and longing,
That I may with your soul unite.

"Make ready your heart's chamber,
Put far all earthly clamor,
Silence all worldly longings now.
Upon you take My quietness,
Eternity's own stillness,
And My approaching footsteps hear.

"Give up your will entirely,
Surrender all completely
To Me, and to My will be given.
Then can I make My dwelling,
Within your heart now reigning,
One then with you in love and pain."

What, then, could be more glorious
Or sweeter than Your presence
Within my heart, O Jesus Christ?
Now all within is silence,

That You may come to enter
My soul, and make it ever Yours.

Yet it is possible to lose the One who has drawn near to us. The Lord can also depart from us if our love for Him grows cold. He will live only in hearts that love Him. Only there does He desire to dwell.

Loving Him means giving Him first place. It means nothing can stir our hearts as He does. We need to be on our guard against being overwhelmed by earth's joys and sorrows, by our work and activities. When such things preoccupy us, Jesus no longer has first place in our lives and has to leave the innermost chamber of our heart, His chosen dwelling-place. Nothing that concerns, excites, or upsets us should be allowed to penetrate into that sanctuary where He lives and has His throne. Ultimately, nothing should disquiet us because He who is our peace is living in the deepest recesses of our heart.

Every true bride of Jesus makes the innermost chamber of her heart a sanctuary. She keeps it holy, for her greatest joy is His promise to make His dwelling in the hearts of those who love Him. For bridal souls, there is no greater fear than losing their first love by being absorbed with the joys and troubles and the ups and downs of daily life. Then Jesus can no longer make His dwelling in their hearts. Filled with trepidation that such a thing might happen, they are careful lest work and pleasure, or even the suffering of others, engross them completely.

The bride of Jesus longs that nothing should drive her Bridegroom from her heart. She knows that He requires of us total devotion: He will not share the throne of our hearts with anyone or anything else. He will not have us dominated by troubles, cares, people, or the things of this world. This is why a bridal soul wholeheartedly resists all such influences that might take control of her. He alone is to reign in her. His indwelling is her greatest joy and happiness. All this means she has a deep inner peace regardless of any external pressures and troubles weighing upon her. She is always one with Him, He in her and she in Him. Thus she goes through life with Him. Everything she does and experiences is in union with Him.

What could be more wonderful than His promise to dwell within us? With Jesus living in the innermost chamber of our heart, what more could we want? He is there even in the darkest night when we feel nothing and He seems far away. What comfort and consolation! Could anything be greater? Even in times of spiritual dryness, that dark night of the soul, we have the assurance: *He who is Life lives in me, and so life will be born in the night.*

Especially in dark times of testing, when troubles threaten to overwhelm us, our heavenly Bridegroom is lovingly and intently watching to see how we stand our ground and endure. Will we prove ourselves truly His bride? This is what He longs to see. For then we are not wrapped up in ourselves, at the mercy of our feelings, our thoughts, our inner conflict. Instead we are relying on His being there, His dwelling within us. Since His presence is greater than troubles and pressures, our trials will only serve to join us more closely to Him.

Even in the darkest hour we can be sure that Jesus is with us, although we cannot feel His presence. What we need to do is commit to Him everything that is burdening us, for this brings us into union with Him, and then He will minister through us.

So even times of spiritual dryness and hardship yield choice fruit.

If we do not wish to go through a dying process,
our love for Jesus will die.
If we choose a dying process,
the divine life of love will blossom
because Jesus will find room in us.

For times of spiritual night, Jesus the Bridegroom has words of encouragement for the soul that loves Him:

Persevere.
Keep up the struggle.
It's worth it.
Remember the heavenly goal.
Am I not enough for you?
Will you not suffer with Me?
Look at Me,
and your hardships will dwindle to nothing.
I am really here. Oh, believe Me!

The bride of Jesus answers: Yes, You are here. What more can I want? Amen.

I love You, Lord, the loveliest and fairest,
And all I am and have is Yours, dear Jesus.
Within my heart You dwell and have Your throne,
O Lamb of God and Bridegroom of my soul,
    Beloved Lamb.

I love You, Lord; You gave Your life to save me,
And now my life, my all, are Yours completely.

I love You, Lord, and yearn to be Your own,
Your very own, dear Lord, all Yours alone,
　　All Yours alone.

I love You, Lord, oh, hear my song of ardor,
My song of love's devotion and deep fervor.
King of my heart, beloved God and Lord,
Your bride is Yours now and forevermore,
　　Forever Yours.

And soon I'll see You face to face, dear Savior,
Awesome in majesty and peerless splendor.
Then from my heart a stream of love will flow
In worship, praise, thanksgiving, wondering awe
　　Unceasingly.

*"Lord Jesus, Your very nearness
brings great peace deep within,
And Your loving gaze,
speaking of grace so infinite,
Fills my soul with joy and thankfulness."*

Christian Gregor
1723–1801

17

Experiencing His Presence

Those with bridal love for Jesus know the bliss of Jesus' drawing near. Their love yearns constantly for such times, for the soul who loves longs to be near the Beloved. We read in the Psalms, "As the deer pants for streams of water, so my soul pants for you, O God. My soul thirsts for God, for the living God" (Psalm 42:1–2 NIV). The wonderful thing is that there are times when we are visited by the love of Jesus. It is a fact that people gripped with bridal love for Jesus have known the intimacy of His divine love in a special way.

Satan and his evil spirits can draw near to people and pervade matter; sometimes, too, their presence can be distinctly felt or even heard in a room. How much more does Jesus perceptibly draw near to those who love Him! He can fill a room with the fragrance of His presence. Also, He can come to us in such a way that we not only sense His presence but He permeates our entire being.

God is eternal, holy, and unapproachable, but according to the witness of Scripture, His love compels Him to reveal His presence to us sinful human beings. From an early stage in Israel's history, the miracle of divine revelation is evident. God calls Himself "I am who I am"—the God who is actively present. With Moses God spoke "face to face, as a man speaks to his friend" (Exodus 33:11), and Moses' face shone because of this close encounter with the holy God (Exodus 34:29). Time and again God revealed Himself, working in people, drawing near in His holiness. The prophet Isaiah, for instance, felt deeply convicted in His presence, exclaiming, "Woe is me! For I am lost . . ." (Isaiah 6:5). We read that the disciple John fell down as though dead at the sight of the glorified Jesus (Revelation 1:17). To this day, an encounter with Jesus as the heavenly Bridegroom can have just as real an impact.

How blessed, how holy is an encounter with the Godhead! It is by far the most profound experience one could ever have. When God meets with a person in this way, that person will never be the same again—he will be transformed. Blessed are those whom God has so touched with His love that they fall down before Him as sinners. Blessed are those whom God has so touched with His love that their hearts burn within them.

Histories of the great lovers of God give a glimpse of this truth. St. Francis of Assisi, for instance, had such a blessed encounter with the triune God that body, soul, and spirit were flooded with the sweetness of Jesus. His face became radiant, so much so that he covered it with his hood. Even if such experiences are the exception rather than the rule, it is still true that Jesus draws near to each bridal soul in His own special way as the heavenly Bridegroom.

Before Your feet, O Lord, I lie adoring.
To greet You, Lord, my soul to heaven is soaring;
You are so fair, so full of tenderness;
My heart is set on fire by all Your loveliness.

To none on earth nor cherubim in heaven
Is knowledge of Your beauty fully given.
Beside it other glories all grow dim.
How blessed am I, for I am greatly loved by Him!

O Jesus, focus of the earthly story,
Resplendent mirror of God's power and glory,
Before You, Lord, in worship now I fall;
For me the vision of Your face is all in all.

*"As the heavens are higher than the earth,
so are my ways higher than your ways and my thoughts
than your thoughts."*

Isaiah 55:9

18

Completely Available for Him

My Lord and heavenly Bridegroom knocked gently at the door of my heart, as if to say, "Give Me more of your time. Give Me more room in your heart. I want you completely." What did the Lord want? Did He want more than my normal times of prayer? I could not escape these persistent questions. Jesus had a claim on my love. I sensed His pleas and longing. He wanted me to enter more fully into His fellowship, to come apart so as to be completely available for Him.

How could I resist Him? He who is Love eternal, the fairest of the sons of men and the divine Majesty, draws near to sinners, desiring their love and devotion. How could I refuse Him? So every day I came apart for a few hours, and the Lord graciously enabled me still to get my work done. Even then His urging did not cease. His love was still not satisfied. So I began to devote every Friday to Him; and, as I tore myself away from my work and other commitments, He rewarded me with a sense of His loving presence such as I had never known before.

I felt His love, burning like a fire and far more intense than any human love, coming straight from the heart of Him whose love sustains the universe. I felt His love, fervent yet gentle, as no human love could be. His love was irresistible, drawing me closer and closer, calling me to be completely available for Him.

If I spent so much time apart with Jesus, would this not be to the neglect of the spiritual daughters entrusted to my care? Would it not place more burdens on Mother Martyria? Would not much of the work He had given me remain unfinished? The Lord taught me that when we abide in Him, loving Him above all else, with all our heart, soul, strength, and mind (Luke 10:27), following wherever He calls us in His love, the richest fruit would come of such union (John 15:5) and those entrusted to us would experience the fullness of blessing.

And this is what happened, contrary to all human thinking. At first my spiritual daughters wept. A few months later, however, they were no longer sad but happy because of the new spiritual life they were experiencing as a result of God's leading for me—the call to seclusion. Now, when we came together, Jesus met with us in a new way, blessing us abundantly. Never before had He been so real to us, whether as the Child in the manger, the Man of Sorrows, or the risen Lord. What my daughters missed on a human level through my absence, Jesus in His love more than made up for, renewing and enriching their lives, making them far happier than before.

And what about my work and activities? Whenever something had to be written, whether a letter or a book, I wrote out of this deeper union with Him, and He was able to touch the hearts of others in a new way. The Lord had once said that from the narrow confines of my room, when I was alone with Him in prayer, the message He had entrusted to us would penetrate further and more effectively than if I had been involved in a normal form of ministry. And now we were privileged to see the writings born of seclusion spread to many parts of the world. Thousands more were reached and blessed by the message the Lord had entrusted to us than if I had been involved in active ministry at Kanaan.

Because Jesus is love, it is a spiritual law that He blesses those He draws to Himself. When He calls upon us to give up the company of loved ones and our former activities, He repays us a hundredfold, as we experienced in our times together as a fellowship with Jesus as the focal point. Much more than that, He gives us new divine life, His love, an ever-flowing river.

19

On the Desert Road

Blissful experiences of Jesus' presence are but a foretaste of what awaits us in heaven. So long as we are on earth, however, the heavenly Bridegroom will, at times, withdraw His perceptible presence, while still dwelling within us. At such times He leads us along dark paths like the bride in the Song of Songs, who comes up from the wilderness "leaning upon her beloved" (Song of Songs 8:5). There are times when the bride of Christ finds that her soul is parched. She seeks for her Beloved, but to no avail. It has become dark in her soul. Still there is no sign of Him. And yet it is precisely then that the heavenly Bridegroom shows how much He loves His bride. Through such experiences He makes His bride more lovely and lovable than before. On the desert road, with her Bridegroom apparently far away, the bride of Christ becomes aware of her wretchedness. It is a humiliating experience. Humbled, she sees her sin and weakness and weeps over them. Her tears are more precious to the

Lord than anything else. We recall the great sinner who washed Jesus' feet with her tears, drawing from Jesus the comment, "She loved much."

This is the kind of generous love for which Jesus longs. He knows that bridal love needs that personal encounter with Him. But because He wants our love for Him to grow, to become purer and stronger, He withdraws from us from time to time. Our soul craves the bliss of His love, but these emotional longings must wither and die. If the bride can still follow the Bridegroom faithfully without being able to feel His presence, then her love is tried and tested. After her trials, she will come up from the wilderness refined and "leaning upon her beloved," who will delight her with His presence.

Profound mysteries and infinite treasures lie buried in the depths of bridal love. Whoever would discover these treasures must dare to plunge into the depths of this ocean. It is the dark night of the soul, the way of the cross, the fellowship of His sufferings that reveal these treasures to us. If Jesus said to James and John, who were eager to share His glory on the throne, "Are you able to drink the cup that I am to drink?" (Matthew 20:22), will He not say to those who long for the blessings of His love and the bliss of spiritual union with Him, "Are you ready to drink the cup of suffering?" Suffering brings glory— and not only in the next life. Whoever goes the way of the cross with Jesus tastes His glory even here and now.

On paths of suffering
When night surrounds me,
I praise the blessing that will come.

I'll suffer willingly—
This will prepare me
To dwell in glory without end.

Suffering will be no more,
Forever transformed
To light and joy at Jesus' throne.

"That I may know him and the power of his resurrection, and the fellowship of his sufferings, being conformed to his death, if, by any means, I may attain to the resurrection from the dead."

Philippians 3:10–11 NKJV

20

The Fellowship of His Sufferings

Nourishing bridal love for Jesus means, above all, meditating on His sufferings. Jesus the heavenly Bridegroom is, and always will be, the Man of Sorrows. In heaven He still bears the scars of His wounds as "the Lamb who was slain" (Revelation 5:12). Because He is the same yesterday, today, and forever, His heart suffers to this day, grieving over our sin. Do Jesus' sufferings have a place in my heart? Does my heart feel for His past and present sufferings? Does my heart ache over His pain today, pain caused by my sin and the sins of the world? This is a test of my love for Jesus.

Before my discovery of bridal love for Jesus, I knew about His sufferings and was often moved by them, but they did not affect me more deeply than that. Then, when I learned to love Jesus, I was given insight into His heart. To this day His heart is filled with sorrow over humanity—believers and nonbelievers alike. Jesus is still suffering, because so many grieve Him by sinning deliberately and because so many Christians bring shame upon His name by living in strife. He suffers because of those who declare Him dead—even within the ranks of the church today. He grieves over all those who hate and mock Him, piercing His heart with malice. He suffers especially when those once close to Him come to prefer people or things and so forsake their first love for Him.

It is the nature of love to offer comfort and relief when seeing someone suffer. This is love's most precious task. If we love and respect someone, we cannot bear to see him dishonored, defamed, and insulted. Not until I learned to love Jesus was my heart on fire to do something loving for Him and to make every effort to encourage love and reverence for Him. Pain for the suffering heart of Jesus moved me to speak and write about His sorrows, so that others would be challenged to give Jesus their love.

The painful realization that God receives little gratitude and worship, even for the glories of His creation, was the motivation for building two small praise chapels to His glory in the Swiss Alps. The sufferings of Jesus were the inspiration for a Garden of Jesus' Sufferings in our land of Kanaan. There the monuments and sculptures depicting the Passion of Christ have helped to make His sufferings from Gethsemane to Calvary come alive for many visitors.

Love is never passive but always comes up with ideas of how to thank Jesus for His past sufferings and how to bring Him comfort in His present-day sufferings. Jesus is the Man of Sorrows. It is impossible to have bridal love for Him without being able to relate to His sufferings. Constantly thanking Jesus for His sufferings, those who love Him also grieve for Him in His pain, entering into the fellowship of His sufferings like a true bride who shares her bridegroom's burdens.

What is the fellowship of His sufferings? Let us look at the life of the apostle Paul. When presenting his credentials as a servant of Christ, he listed the trials he experienced in following Jesus, such as poverty, deprivation, physical danger, humiliation, hunger, disappointments, and loss of reputation (2 Corinthians 11:23–28).

At the beginning of my walk with Jesus as my heavenly Bridegroom, I was aware of Him as the lonely and forsaken One. It was as though He were asking me, *Will you come with Me and share My life of suffering and all that it entails? Will you share My poverty, self-renunciation, disgrace, and lowliness?* Entering the fellowship of His sufferings is a matter of love. Love willingly treads the path of the Bridegroom, even if it is a thorny one. Here, love for Jesus is seen in action. If we go this way, we nourish bridal love and become more and more closely joined to Jesus. This is what I found after saying yes to Jesus and going the way of the cross with Him.

The Lord really did let me taste something of His sufferings as I followed Him. I experienced derision, slander, hatred, and disgrace for His name's sake. He let me taste the suffering that accompanies poverty. Poverty is humbling, leaving you dependent upon others, without money, rights, and influence in the eyes of the world, apparently helpless when it comes to achieving something for the kingdom of God. I discovered what it is like to go without food and sleep for His sake. But I also found that the fellowship of His sufferings leads to the fellowship of His love. Words cannot describe how close Jesus came to me on this path, overwhelming me with His love. This is why it is called the *fellowship* of His sufferings. Suffering borne with Jesus leads us into close fellowship with Him, a union of love.

To each one who desires to be a bridal soul, Jesus draws near as the Man of Sorrows. Even today He suffers anguish of heart as He is mocked, defamed, humiliated, and forsaken. We can almost hear Him asking, *Who will come with Me? I am so alone. Who will be My bride and companion? Who will share My sufferings? Who will share My humiliation, disgrace, lowliness, and poverty?*

This is how the fellowship of His sufferings begins. For many in our times it will end in martyrdom. Times of persecution demonstrate most clearly that the fellowship of His sufferings is the fellowship of His love. We know that the flame of love burned brightly in countless numbers persecuted for His name's sake; by their words and actions they proved that one force is greater than the most terrible suffering: love for Jesus. They were a living testimony of the Scripture, "Love is strong as death" (Song of Songs 8:6). Love is stronger than anything else, because it is immortal. Love triumphs over all sufferings and trials, even torture, and brings victorious joy.

We are approaching an age of martyrdom. For years Christians have suffered under repressive regimes, while in nominally Christian countries new legislation makes it increasingly difficult to uphold Christian values. Antagonism toward Christianity will spread throughout the world, as prophesied by Jesus for the end times: "You will be hated by all nations for my name's sake" (Matthew 24:9). This is why it is vital for us to have bridal love for Jesus and to know the fellowship of His sufferings. Without this bridal love we will not have the strength to endure for His sake.

Many examples could be given of Christians who, in times of testing, either denied Jesus or forsook Him. Why? Previously they had failed to enter into the fellowship of His sufferings. In earlier days, they had been unwilling to bear suffering or to make sacrifices for the Lord. Jesus meant less to them than career, income, prestige, or family. Faced with martyrdom, such people failed utterly, breaking down in despair. Their lives radiated nothing of the joy of the early Christians.

It is written that those who love Him will receive the crown of life (James 1:12). Those who love Jesus are overcomers even in the deepest suffering and martyrdom. Even if we were to sell all our possessions to gain this love (Song of Songs 8:7), it would still be too little, for this love is without price. Because Jesus knows what He is offering us, He can call upon us to take up our cross and to share in the fellowship of His sufferings. He knows that He is offering eternal life in return. He knows that He will repay us a hundred times over for everything we forsake out of love when we follow Him on the way of the cross. There will be reward in this life but even more so in the glory of heaven.

> With You the cross' way I'll go,
> With You I'll share its pain and woe,
> With You go into darkness.
> With You I will one day arise
> And reign with You in Paradise,
> With You I am united.

With You I'll suffer pain and death,
With You will draw my last slow breath,
While dying, ever living.
With You I'll know the joy of love,
With You I'll soar to heaven above
And taste life everlasting.

With You I'll live from hour to hour
And find Your love has healing power
Each time my heart is wounded.
With You I'll love the long, dark night,
For it will bring me heaven's light,
With You light conquers darkness.

With You I'll bear the sense of loss,
With You I'll suffer any cross,
So I Your heart may enter.
With You I will accept all this,
For it will bring me glorious bliss,
The love of God eternal.

"God, the Spouse of my soul,
God, who makes my soul fruitful for eternal life—
Him alone will I love and nothing other than Him."

St. Augustine
354–430

21

Mirror of Conscience

When do you have "first love" for Jesus?

You have first love for Jesus when you lovingly pronounce the name of Jesus in your heart—whether consciously or unconsciously—and keep finding new names for Him: my Beloved, my Treasure, my Life, my Joy, my One and All.

When you are compelled to worship Jesus your Bridegroom simply for who He is—and when your heart never loses that sense of awe and wonder.

When your heart can and must sing for joy, "Called to be a bride of Jesus!"

When you daily come with tears of contrition to the cross, filled with love and gratitude for His forgiveness and for what He has done for you through His suffering and death.

When you desire nothing else but to be loved by Him.

When He alone captivates you; when only His presence fills you with overwhelming joy.

When even during leisure your first thought is of Jesus and to spend time with Him rather than seeking the company of others or pursuing your favorite pastime.

When you are moved to endure suffering or to give up something for His sake; when you keep thinking of new ways to give Him gifts.

When faced with the choice between Him and people or things you love, you choose Him without further reflection.

When you go about your daily work with Him.

When you gladly and lovingly bear trials, constantly affirming, *For You, for You.*

When Jesus truly is the joy of your heart and when your face and whole personality are radiant with this joy.

When nothing makes you so happy as knowing that Jesus is receiving love and glory from people and that His kingdom is being extended.

When you seek to please Him rather than to please others.

When you no longer do anything for your own gratification, pleasure, and glory, but rather work to bring Him joy and glory.

When you completely surrender your will and wishes to Him.

When you keep thinking of ways to make Jesus happy by worshiping Him in prayer and song, by spending yourself in His service, by showing love to others for His name's sake, by willingly making little sacrifices as occasion arises.

When you ardently long for the day when you see Him face to face and are united with Him forever.

When you have no idols in your heart—people or things you love as much as you love Jesus or even more than you love Him. Jesus accepts only undivided love.

When you trust Him, as a bride trusts her bridegroom, saying, "He is with me. He protects me. He stands up for me. He does everything for me. He cares for me. He has my best interests at heart."

When you have a closer relationship with Jesus than with anyone else, no matter how dear.

When Jesus is the great Love of your heart and life.

When losing everything that makes life meaningful for you, you can say, "So long as I have You, I have all I need."

When for love of Him you wholeheartedly resist sin, so that He can make you a beautiful bride to His joy.

When confronted with your sin, you weep for having grieved and disappointed Him.

When you follow Him unconditionally and uncompromisingly, just as a true bride shares the life of her bridegroom.

When, in spite of the pain, you lovingly and joyfully follow the path of poverty, lowliness, humiliation, obedience, dependence, purity, suffering, and self-denial, knowing that His life was no different, and welcoming every aspect of the discipleship of the cross as a sign that you belong to Him.

When you cannot bear the thought of His being grieved without wanting to share His pain and to comfort Him by doing something that will bring Him joy.

When you are moved to worship Him for His wounds, which tell of His sacrificial, suffering love—His essential nature.

When you are always waiting: waiting for His visit in everyday life, waiting for His presence, and waiting for the day He comes for His bride to celebrate the marriage supper of the Lamb.

> But I have this against you, that you have abandoned the love you had at first. Remember then from what you have fallen, repent and do the works you did at first. (Revelation 2:4–5)

When do I not love Him as I did at first?

When I let cares enter my heart and lodge there, they smother the flame of bridal love.

When I harbor accusations against my neighbor in my heart and nurse such feelings, they choke bridal love.

When I seek my own satisfaction and glory in my activities and service, bridal love disappears from my heart.

When I am not ready to commit my will to Jesus, He withdraws from me and my love dies.

When I am not willing to own up to my sin and to humble myself, I lose His grace; without the experience of His forgiveness, my love withers away.

When I rebel against chastening and suffering, my love-relationship to Jesus is disrupted. I no longer love Him as I first did.

When the things of this world, a person or object, become my idol, the focus of my thoughts and love, I have abandoned my first love.

When my best time, my greatest energy, my attention, and inclinations are centered on someone or something other than Jesus, bridal love dies.

When something totally absorbs me, Jesus is excluded. The bridal relationship is disrupted, and I don't love Him as I did.

When I no longer live according to God's commandments,

I show that I do not love the One who gave them, and my bridal relationship is marred.

When I am no longer grieved by my sinning, I do not belong to my Bridegroom, the Friend and Savior of sinners. The union of love is broken. The flame of bridal love is about to die.

When I no longer hate my sin and fight it, I do not love Him who died for my sin. The bridal relationship is disrupted.

When I tolerate possessiveness, envy, hatred, resentment, impurity, lies, self-centeredness in my life, I am shut out from the kingdom of God and shut off from Jesus. My bridal love withers and dies.

When I am taken up more with earthly things, everyday life, my work, my joys, and sorrows, rather than with heavenly things, I become estranged from my Bridegroom Jesus, the King of heaven. My bridal love dies away.

When I doubt Jesus' love, help, and victory, my union with Him is disrupted and bridal love grows dim.

When I become resentful of my cross and the sacrifices required of me, this is a sign that my love for Jesus is at the point of death, for love enables us gladly to sacrifice for the Beloved.

When I am spiritually lukewarm and smug, no longer yearning to hear about Jesus and to worship Him as a true bride longs to hear about her bridegroom, then I am no longer a bride. I have lost the love I had at first.

When I am not dismayed and grieved that His body is divided, that He is dishonored, that His name is blasphemed, that He is not loved, then I show that I am not a bride of Jesus. My bridal love has died.

How can I bring joy to my Bridegroom Jesus?

> She has done a beautiful thing to me . . . She did what she could. (Mark 14:6–8 NIV)

To make Jesus happy and comfort Him—is such a thing possible? Yes, indeed. Just as we can grieve God's heart (Genesis 6:6), so we can also bring Him joy and comfort, especially when He is grieved. In the book of Psalms it's as if Jesus Himself were speaking to us: "I looked . . . for comforters, but I found none" (Psalm 69:20). But how do we become comforters? Perhaps we look to great deeds and sacrifices as a means of bringing Him joy and comfort, while failing to recognize that daily living itself gives ample opportunity for this expression of love to Jesus.

I bring joy and comfort to my Bridegroom Jesus when I can say in suffering, "I want to bear this suffering out of love and gratitude to You."

When plagued by fear, I declare, "I trust You. You have conquered my fear."

When all seems dead within me and I affirm, "You are my Life."

When sensing my bondage to sin, I still say, "You are my Redeemer. I believe in Your victory."

When I am prepared to come to the cross, knowing myself to be a sinner in the sight of God and man.

When I do not despair in the midst of failure but continue to sing of His sacrifice, for He has done everything to set me free.

When faced with great difficulties, I say, "My troubles cannot be greater than You, my Helper."

When following a difficult leading, I say, "I know that You will make the bitter sweet."

When I declare during great inner conflict, "I will cling to You and follow You to the end. I trust in Your love."

When I declare during times of spiritual night and God-forsakenness, "Nothing can separate me from You. I am knit together with You."

When I declare on paths of chastening, "Thank You, Jesus. You are my heavenly Bridegroom. In Your love You want to bless me through chastening and prepare me for the heavenly glory."

When I say while very busy, "I love You, Jesus."

When I say, "Thank You, Lord" every time demands are made on me during the day and the work load increases.

When feeling burdened, I say, "I will bear the load gladly for You and with You."

When I love my cross.

When I celebrate His victory in the midst of my defeat.

When His sufferings, rather than my own, fill my heart.

When I spend time in prayer lovingly contemplating His sufferings.

When I am eager to hear what He has to say to me.

When, for love of Him, I do someone a good turn.

When, rather than complain, I am thankful, knowing that He always has my best interests at heart.

When I think more about His concerns than about my own.

When I speak words of love to Him even in times of spiritual dryness.

When I spend myself in saving souls and kindling them with love for Him.

When I sacrifice time, money, strength, and prestige to spread the glory of His name.

When I do not forget the good things He has done for me but count my blessings with gratitude.

When I accept His wishes, His will, and His commandments as holy and binding, surrendering my will and wishes to Him.

When I seek only to please Him rather than win the approval, love, and esteem of others.

When I desire only what He desires, accepting that it is His to give and His to withhold.

When I bear witness to Him, His love, and His sufferings.

When I bring Him my adoration in word or in song.

When I offer Him a sacrifice of love.

When there is darkness within and around me but I say, "You are my Light, which nothing can extinguish."

When I proclaim in hopeless situations, "You are the Way. You have made a path for me. I trust You."

When I forgive those who have hurt me or wronged me, as He has forgiven me.

When I bear with difficult people in love and patience, just as He always bears with me.

When I show kindness to those who make life hard for me, always remembering how kind God is to me.

When, for love of Him, I gladly do things that I find hard.

When I constantly think about Him and tell Him how much I love Him.

When humiliated and disgraced, I still thank Him for the privilege of sharing His path.

When I prefer Him to all else—people, things, pleasures—because He is the joy of my heart.

When neither cares nor sorrows can drive Him from my heart.

When I humble myself before God and man.

When I trust in His love in every situation.

"I came to cast fire upon the earth; and would that it were already kindled!"

Luke 12:49

22

On Fire for God

The love of a bridal soul for Jesus is like a flaming fire. It burns with great intensity like "a most vehement flame" (Song of Songs 8:6). Why is this so? The bride of Christ loves the One most worthy of love, the fairest of all, for whom she feels inwardly constrained to spend herself. She is so gripped by His wishes that she does everything to fulfill them. And what is it that He desires? "To cast fire upon the earth" (Luke 12:49). He desires that redemption will come to those in bondage, that people will be led back to their heavenly Father. He desires that His kingdom will come, that it will make headway in every nation. He desires spiritual fires to be lit everywhere, so that something of God's dominion, His rule, the kingdom of heaven, will be seen in this dark world.

The concerns of Jesus' heart encompass the whole world, and so He has entrusted His bride with a worldwide commission. Zeal for those concerns for which He gave His life burns in His heart. He would kindle such a fire in every true bride, inspiring her to spend her life so that souls are saved and His kingdom is extended.

Bridal love for Jesus
is ever active,
always pressing on
with a growing sense of urgency,
ever lavishing gifts on the Beloved,
ever spending itself for Him.
Love is the opposite
of smugness and complacency.

Those kindled with bridal love work zealously for the advance of the kingdom of God. Never content with the *status quo*, they constantly set themselves new goals of faith, because everything they have so far achieved for their Bridegroom seems insufficient. They long to see Him receive more love and glory. They stir up individuals and groups, rousing them from a selfish absorption with personal sanctification, inspiring them to focus on the Lover of their souls and to spend themselves for His concerns and His glory.

People on fire with bridal love are always alert and ready to spend time and energy carrying their Bridegroom's consuming love further afield. In faith they seize every opportunity to conquer new areas. Their master is the King of Kings, whose domain is the entire universe. Consequently, "the world is their parish," and their hearts are large enough to identify with the needs and suffering of the whole world. Knowing that the Bridegroom has come to establish the kingdom of heaven on earth, and having tasted it personally in fellowship with Him, the bride will not rest until she can see its advance in this dark world. Nothing less satisfies her. She uses every hour and wastes no time. She willingly treads paths of repentance, deepest humiliation, and suffering, if only the way be paved for the kingdom of God. And she is aware that she can bring the kingdom of God to others only if a sense of her own importance does not stand in the way.

Wherever she goes, the bride of Jesus reflects something of heaven's radiance. Aflame with love for her Bridegroom, she sparks off fires in the hearts of others. Such is the nature of the bride, for no one is a bride of Jesus who does not have a burning love and zeal for the kingdom of God.

Yet the zeal of the bride does not come from herself; like everyone else, she is a sinful human being. However, she lives in union with Him who is ablaze with love and who has become her Bridegroom. With Him she treads the path of self-denial, which leads to spiritual life and to a foretaste of heaven. At His side she shares in this life. In obedience she has let go of everything else to walk with Him who is her all and all. This is why she does not have to rely on self, talent, personality, resources, or opportunities. She reckons exclusively with Him and with the power of His love. Jesus is the very fire of God, the Light of the world, a furnace of love. As such He cannot fail to inflame the heart of His bride.

Oh, that Your fire would soon be kindled,
Emerging from Your love divine,
And that the whole world soon acknowledge
Your majesty as King sublime!
—George Friedrich Fickert (1758–1815)

"One thing alone do I desire—
Were it mine,
I would count all else as loss—
To be united with You forever, O Lord,
A sacrifice of love, accepted by grace."

Rudolf Alexander Schröder
1878–1962

23

Kindling the Flame of Bridal Love

Bridal love is kindled the more you contemplate Jesus, your heavenly Bridegroom, the more you think about Him, the more your heart converses with Him, the more your tongue declares who He is. Turn your eyes upon Jesus. Meditate especially on Him as the Man of Sorrows, for in His sufferings the fullness of His beauty is revealed. Proclaim who your heavenly Bridegroom is and what He is like, praise Him in song, and your heart will be kindled to love Him all the more. The more you come to know Him and the wonders of His love, the more you are irresistibly drawn to love Him in return.

Bridal love is kindled through every fresh encounter with your Bridegroom as you speak with Him. Seek frequent encounters with Jesus. The more you use every possible moment for prayer, to meet with Him, to talk with Him, to pour out your heart to Him, and to hear what He is saying to you, the more your love grows.

Bridal love is kindled when you make more room in your heart for Jesus by removing whatever displeases Him, whatever you cling to. Make room for Him so that He can dwell in your heart and pour out His love. It is a matter of letting go of your dearest and best, so that you gain the dearest of all, your heavenly Bridegroom.

Bridal love is kindled through dedication. Whenever you surrender something to Jesus, the bond of love with Him becomes stronger. Surrendering your will and wishes entails sacrifice; but the more you sacrifice for Jesus, the more closely you will be knit to Him. Your love will be set aflame every time you align your will with His, for love always grows stronger through union. Yes, the flame of love burns brightly as we sacrifice our will upon the altar.

Bridal love is kindled when you stay close to Jesus, your heavenly Bridegroom, sharing His pathway. You will be joined more closely to Him every time you set foot on the stepping-stones of His pathway: poverty, lowliness, hardship, humility, obedience, and purity. But as soon as you set foot on a stepping-stone other than His, you separate yourself from Him. All your worship of Him, all your talk of bridal love, will be to no avail. The flame of bridal love will die.

Bridal love is kindled when you trust in Jesus, your heavenly Bridegroom. Trust is honoring to Him. It causes Him to draw close to you in love, and this, in turn, inflames your love. Offer Him your trust especially when it is dark in your heart, when He no longer answers, when He seems far away and unconcerned about you. Trust in His love when you can no longer understand His leadings, your hopes are dashed, and everything appears meaningless. If then you can still trust Him and say, "You are with me. You are in my heart. We are united forever. Nothing and no one can separate us," then this steadfastness in loving trust will make your flame of love burn brightly. Your bridal love will have stood the test.

Bridal love is kindled when you do everything with Jesus. Throughout each day do even the smallest, most insignificant and ordinary things with Him. Then you will find that everything done in union with Him inspires a new love, a constant love, a love that is dear to Him, because it proves its genuineness in everyday life. Practice doing everything with Him all day long.

Bridal love is kindled when you do everything for His sake, devoting special love and attention to the difficult tasks. If the words *for You* spring from the heart, especially when you are finding a task or leading difficult, then the flame of love is revived.

Bridal love is kindled when you come to the cross in repentance. Lack of repentance quenches the flame of love. Repentance fans it into flame. Repentance is fuel for love's fire, making it burn brightly. Repentance opens our eyes to see Jesus as the Man of Sorrows, wounded because of our sins. Repentance renders our suffering Savior beautiful in our sight, inspiring us with new love. Only tears shed over our sin open our eyes to see Jesus in His loveliness. If your eyes are tearless, you may be able to speak much about Him, but you will not see Him with your heart and really love Him.

Bridal love is kindled when sorrow over sin moves you to repentance and restores you to fellowship with Jesus. Just as you once grieved Him with your sinning, so now contrition will lead you to find some way of bringing Him joy. His joy over what you do will fill your heart and increase your love for Him. Every act of repentance adds fuel to the fire of love.

Bridal love is kindled when, as a bride, you reflect on the essential nature of your heavenly Bridegroom—His love. That love suffers still in its longing for the lost. Meditate upon Jesus' Passion and the anguish He feels today. Such meditation will cause your love to grow both in fervency and in tenderness. You will feel for Jesus and enter into His pain. Inspired to bring Him comfort, you will be willing even to endure suffering if that would refresh Him.

Bridal love is kindled when you live in expectation of Jesus' second coming. The bride's heart is flooded with the joy of anticipation. If this joy is missing, however, our love grows dim. Await your King and Bridegroom, who is coming again in glory and who will escort His bride to that heavenly celebration, the marriage supper of the Lamb. If His coming occupies your thoughts, you will also sing and speak of it. Then, here and now, He will make His dwelling in your heart and your love will grow. Day by day expect Him, for daily He longs to draw near. Also wait for Him to come and take you home to Himself at the end of your life, when He will receive you in love and you will see Him face to face.

Bridal love is kindled as you pronounce His name. The more a bride utters her bridegroom's name, the more ardent her love becomes. Say, "Jesus, Jesus, Jesus," throughout the day and in the night should you awake. His name has the power to kindle the love of His bride. Never forget there is power in saying a name, and the greatest power of all lies in saying the name of Jesus. When His name is pronounced, He draws near in love, for He loves those who love Him. And love always expresses itself by lovingly saying the name of the beloved.

Bridal love is kindled when you come apart with the Lord. Only in times of quiet and solitude, when a bride and her bridegroom are alone, can they fully give their love to one another. Only in privacy can they gaze at each other lovingly and utter words of love. A delicate veil hangs over lovers. Their love is not for public display but for when they are alone. Seek, then, times of quietness when no one can disturb you, when everything around you is silent, when there is nothing to distract you, and when you can devote yourself completely to Jesus. Believe that He will draw near. Believe that He is present and will speak to your heart. Only those who dare to come apart and who have the courage to go through times of spiritual dryness as well will know His loving presence in such a way that their love will burst into flame.

> *"Thus says the Lord,*
> *I remember the devotion of your youth,*
> *your love as a bride,*
> *how you followed me in the wilderness."*

> Jeremiah 2:2

24

Jesus and the Loving Soul

HIS PLEDGE:
I love you as no human being possibly could.
I give you everything you need.
I care for you as no human being ever could.
I will not be deterred by your sin, for I love you and
have come to show sinners the right way.
I tell you My innermost concerns, for you are My bride.
When you are one with Me, nothing is too hard for you.
One day I will present you to My Father a glorious bride.

HIS PLEA:
Let My love be sufficient for you.
Surrender your will to Me as the greatest token of your love.
Let My eyes guide you.

Let all else be silent so that I may speak.

Listen today for a wish of Mine.

Rest in My heart.

Bring Me joy with your worship.

Proclaim Me, your heavenly Bridegroom, in every way you can.

Show kindness to your neighbor, and you show kindness to me.

Keep your eyes focused on Me, and you will be kindled with love.

Love Me in whatever way I come to you and deal with you.

Love Me as your Judge.

Love Me even in times of spiritual dryness;
be faithful to Me then.

Love Me by obeying Me in everyday life.

Meditate on My sufferings, and you will discover My heart.

Give Me your love by loving your cross.

HIS CHALLENGE:

If you want Me, choose My path of lowliness and disgrace.

If you want Me, do not be self-seeking; seek not the fulfillment of your wishes but the fulfillment of My will.

HIS ASSURANCES:

Are you in the wilderness? I will be everything to you.

Are you in spiritual darkness? I will be your Light.

Are you bound in sins? I will be your Redeemer.

Are you perplexed? I will be your Counselor.

Are you feeling sad? I will give you laughter.

Are you plagued by fears? I will shelter you in My love.

Are you in distress? I will carry you through.

"What do I love when I love You? Not physical beauty,
nor the glamour of the world, nor the brilliant light of day
so pleasing to the eye, nor sweet melodies of intricate songs,
nor the fragrance of flowers and perfumes, nor manna, nor
honey ... these are not the things I love when I love You,
my God. And yet I love You as though You were light
and sweet scent and melody and food and the fulfillment
of my spiritual desires! Within my soul there shines a
light which the world cannot comprehend; there ring
melodies which do not fade with the passing of time;
there sweet scents are wafted that no wind can disperse;
there the taste of food will never lead to satiety;
there the bliss of united love will never cloy.
All this I love when I love my God."

St. Augustine
354–430

25

Jesus' Incomparable Love

Jesus' love is so tender and blissful that He can make His bride completely happy.

Jesus' love is so overflowing that He can shower His bride with gifts and blessings.

Jesus' love is so attentive that He responds to every wish and plea of His bride, fulfilling her requests even when it does not seem so to her.

Jesus' love is so strong and passionate that it can revive the heart of His bride when it is apathetic, cold, and lifeless, rekindling it with love.

Jesus' love is so radiant that it fills the heart of His bride with joy, refreshing her when she is sad.

Jesus' love is so long-suffering that He never gives up on His bride but is always patient with her in her sins and troubles.

Jesus' love is so bountiful that it can fulfill all His bride's longings for love.

Jesus' love is so individual that He loves His bride as though she were the only person in the world and He could not exist without her.

Jesus' love is so sympathetic that He always feels for His bride. There is nothing she suffers without His sharing the pain with her.

Jesus' love is so patient that He can wait until the heart of His bride is ready and her love mature enough for all that He will ask of her.

Jesus' love is so forgiving that He covers the sins and shortcomings of His bride when she brings them to the cross.

Jesus' love is so generous that He shares with His bride all that is His, enabling her to share in His very being and His blessings.

Jesus' love is so wonderful that it lacks neither fire nor gentleness, neither strength nor tenderness, neither holiness nor intimacy.

Jesus' love is so heavenly that it grants His bride a foretaste of the bliss of heaven even in this life.

Jesus' love is so unique, a holy love, allowing His bride to live in the realm of His holiness.

Jesus' love is so honorable that He can never disappoint anyone, let alone His bride.

Jesus' love is so sensitive and understanding that He sees the slightest anxieties and emotions of His bride and can refresh her with His love.

"Let us rejoice and exult and give him the glory, for the marriage of the Lamb has come, and his Bride has made herself ready."

Revelation 19:7

26

When the Bridegroom Comes

During a time of ministry in India, I was once awakened at two in the morning by the sound of loud music coming from a neighboring village. It went on until daybreak. Why the noise? In the middle of the night a bridegroom had come for his bride. The whole village received him with music in a mood of joyful celebration. Heart throbbing, the bride had waited for that moment of her bridegroom's coming to take her to her new home, there to be always at his side.

A wonderful illustration of what happens in the spiritual realm! Can we imagine what it will be like when Jesus comes as Bridegroom? That day really is coming. All heaven will ring with the sound of music and rejoicing as a magnificent reception is prepared for the return of the Bridegroom with His bride to their heavenly home. Knowing that He is coming, the bride of Jesus waits expectantly with beating heart. She keeps imagining what it will be like to spend eternity at Jesus' side, completely one with Him. Did He not promise that she would be at His side forever? Even when He takes His seat upon His throne as King of Kings, she will not have to leave His presence; rather He will share His throne with her (Revelation 3:21).

Did He not promise to share with His bride the awesome responsibility of judging the world and the angels (1 Corinthians 6:2–3) and that she would have authority over the nations with Him (Revelation 2:26–27)? Only the bride has the right to share the life of the Bridegroom in eternity. What a destiny awaits the bride of the Lamb!

Are you a bride of the Lamb? His bride carries a wonderful secret in her heart. She has a blessed hope. She lives in expectation of the fulfillment of her deepest longings. She knows that eternal joy and happiness will be hers. This is why the bride needs little else in this life. The test of whether I am a true bride of Jesus is this: How important to me is the love of others? To what extent do I look to my career for satisfaction? Do I covet prestige and status? Do health, talents, and popularity mean more to me than Jesus? The true bride of Jesus is focused on Him in her innermost being rather than on the things of this world. Her Bridegroom is her life, the joy of her heart. Supremely happy in His love, she is enthralled by her heavenly Bridegroom, spending herself for Him, eagerly awaiting His coming, and carrying in her heart this one name: Jesus.

"Dearest Lord Jesus, come soon to reign,"
Hear my voice pleading again and again.
"Come quickly, Lord," is the cry of Your bride.
"I yearn to see You, and with You abide."

My heart is singing one ceaseless song,
"Jesus, my Bridegroom, why are You so long?
Come soon, come quickly, why do You delay?
I look and long for You, Lord, night and day."

The rapturous moment will come at last,
The cry resounding, "The long wait is past!"
Jesus as Bridegroom will soon reappear,
In love unite with the bride He holds dear.

Moment by moment I wait and yearn.
"Oh, won't You whisper when You will return?
My heart will leap then in love to Your side,
O my Beloved, my treasure and pride."

"The Spirit and the Bride say, 'Come.' ... He who testifies to these things says, 'Surely I am coming soon.' Amen. Come, Lord Jesus!"

Revelation 22:17, 20

27

Vigilance—A Mark of the Bride

Nourishing bridal love means being vigilant, always on the alert for Jesus, our heavenly Bridegroom. Blessed were the five virgins who were watchful even while asleep. They were ready to meet the bridegroom and take part in the wedding (Matthew 25:10). But how does the bride of Jesus watch while sleeping, so that she not only awakens when her Bridegroom comes at midnight but is also ready for Him at that late hour?

Only love will keep her vigilant—the love that God, who first loved us, has poured into our hearts through the Holy Spirit. Being born of God, this love has within it the seed of divine life. It is immortal and indestructible and never sleeps. And so the heart of the bride is awake even when she sleeps (Song of Songs 5:2).

Love is awake within the heart of the bride of Jesus, no matter what darkness may surround her, no matter how great the danger of being overcome with sleep. This love is like a sensitive instrument. A single string plucked by the One she loves sounds in her heart, and immediately the bride is awake. Rising quickly, she rushes to meet Him. She would never miss those times when her Bridegroom draws near; for her, such encounters are a foretaste of heaven. So she will not sleep through the hour when the Bridegroom comes in glory to take His bride to Himself and to celebrate with her the marriage supper of the Lamb.

If you want to be a bride of the Lamb ready to go out to meet the Bridegroom when He comes, then take care that this love is alive in you. Do not let it fade, but rather let it keep you spiritually alive and alert. Without this love, you will not be ready when He comes at midnight. Only if divine love burns in your heart can you awaken in a state of readiness, shaking off the paralyzing sleep that will overcome all humanity, believers and nonbelievers alike.

The midnight hour is near. The signs Jesus spoke about in Matthew 24 are being fulfilled. Love is growing cold in many. God's commandments are widely rejected. The onward march of lawlessness is causing devastation and despair. Blasphemy is on the rise, indicating a burning hatred of Jesus Christ. In many parts of the world Christians are suffering for their faith. God's chosen people are returning to the land of their fathers. The Gospel is being preached throughout the world. The Bridegroom is preparing to meet His own. But for whom will He open the door to the banqueting hall, where the marriage supper of the Lamb is to be celebrated on that glorious day of union between the heavenly Bridegroom and His bride, when heaven resounds with the sound of singing and rejoicing? Those for whom love for Jesus is a way of life will see that door open.

Use what time is left. Open your heart wide so that love for Jesus can flow in and shape your life; then, even while you sleep, this love is actively present—simply because your whole being is given over to Him. Do not tolerate anything that would diminish your love for Jesus and cause Him to withdraw His love from you. Do not tolerate a negative attitude toward any person. Do not tolerate any false attachments to people and things. Do not tolerate anything that would draw you away from Jesus' path of lowliness, poverty, disgrace, and obedience. Resist the temptation to go your own way, gratifying self. Be on your guard against losing the love you had at first.

The hour is coming when the One whom your soul loves will appear, but you will not notice if you are not aglow with first love. Nor will you be drawn to Him, for only those who love Him with first love will be drawn to the Bridegroom. In that hour it will be too late to open your heart so that it may be filled afresh with love for Jesus, too late to buy the oil of love. Your heart must already be filled with this love. You must be a bride with all your being so that He will receive you as such when He comes for His bride. He will take as His bride only those who loved Him ardently, even in the darkest moments, and who were ready because their lamps were filled with the oil of repentance and love.

O day of supreme happiness when Jesus celebrates the marriage supper of the Lamb with His bride amid the rejoicing of heaven! It is worth sacrificing everything to gain bridal love, the pearl of great price, in order to know the joy of that day. Yet even if we were to give up everything in this life that is desirable and satisfying for body, soul, and spirit for the sake of this love, we would still have given too little. Attaining the supreme goal of the marriage supper of the Lamb is worth everything.

Know that the midnight hour is approaching, and with it the marriage supper of the Lamb. The Bridegroom is coming. Turn your back on everything that would hinder you from going to meet Him. Live only to love Him.

The holy hour is coming,
When from the heavenly throne
God's Son, who was incarnate,
Will come to claim His own.

He waits with love expectant
For His beloved bride.
Her life to Him she's given;
With bonds of love she's tied.

She hastens quickly to Him
With joy and heavenly bliss,
In every way preparing,
To be completely His.

For through the blood of Jesus,
She now may walk in white,
Attain the heavenly wedding,
His realm of purest light.

The midnight hour is striking,
And dawn no longer far.
So keep a constant vigil,
Soon shines the morning star.

Oh, live then for His advent.
The trumpet sound is near,
Announcing He is coming.
At last the day is here!

"Lo, I am with you always, to the close of the age."

Matthew 28:20

28

Day by Day

1. Someone's always with me—I'm never alone
   Helping and sustaining, for I am His own:
   Jesus, my heavenly Bridegroom.

2. Someone never ceases to love and to care;
   With Him by my side I will go anywhere:
   Jesus, my heavenly Bridegroom.

3. Someone's love envelops me so tenderly;
   Someone sees my sorrow and knows when I'm grieved:
   Jesus, my heavenly Bridegroom.

4. Someone's there who knows how to comfort my soul,
   Someone's always waiting, His love to make known:
   Jesus, my heavenly Bridegroom.

5. Someone's ever with me, so constant and true,
   Gentle and supportive, my soul to renew:
   Jesus, my heavenly Bridegroom.

6. Someone understands when I'm feeling distressed,
   Never far away during anguish and stress:
   Jesus, my heavenly Bridegroom.

7. Someone's always listening, alert to my cries,
   Lovingly aware of my heart's faintest sighs:
   Jesus, my heavenly Bridegroom.

8. Someone's always ready to bring me relief,
   Standing close beside me in hardship and grief:
   Jesus, my heavenly Bridegroom.

9. Someone's hand is lovingly guiding me on,
   Graciously protecting when threatened by harm:
   Jesus, my heavenly Bridegroom.

10. Someone's always lovingly thinking of me,
    Caring and supportive in all of my needs:
    Jesus, my heavenly Bridegroom.

11. Someone's always waiting to see if I'll come,
    To be reunited with Him whom I love:
    Jesus, my heavenly Bridegroom.

12. Someone's there who loves me so intimately,
    Ever reaching out in His longing for me:
    Jesus, my heavenly Bridegroom.

13. Someone outshines all, none with Him can compare.
    None as great as He can be found anywhere:

Jesus, my heavenly Bridegroom.

14. Someone will remain when all things cease to be,
    Someone ever waiting in heaven for me:
    Jesus, my heavenly Bridegroom.

15. Someone's always planning new joys and relief,
    Someone hurting for me and sharing my grief:
    Jesus, my heavenly Bridegroom.

16. Someone understands what is burdening me,
    Someone sees and counts every tear that I weep:
    Jesus, my heavenly Bridegroom.

17. Someone's there whose love for me always avails,
    Someone who will never forsake, never fail:
    Jesus, my heavenly Bridegroom.

18. Someone loves and bears with me just as I am;
    All my sins are washed in the blood of the Lamb:
    Jesus, my heavenly Bridegroom.

19. Someone watches zealously over my soul,
    Purging all the dross till I shine like pure gold:
    Jesus, my heavenly Bridegroom.

20. Someone died at Calvary my soul to redeem
    From the bonds of Satan and sin's tyranny:
    Jesus, my heavenly Bridegroom.

21. Someone suffers with me in deep sympathy,
    Seeking to console me in trouble and in grief:
    Jesus, my heavenly Bridegroom.

22. Someone cares about me, just wanting the best,
    That I might be strengthened and daily refreshed:
    Jesus, my heavenly Bridegroom.

23. Someone cares about me, forgets not my needs,
    Someone who does listen, my every cry heeds:
    Jesus, my heavenly Bridegroom.

24. Someone's love is healing and warm like the sun,
    Welcoming and soothing to everyone:
    Jesus, my heavenly Bridegroom.

25. Someone's planned my future so lovingly
    And prepared a dwelling in heaven for me:
    Jesus, my heavenly Bridegroom.

26. Someone's waiting daily for proofs of my love,
    Words of deep affection as one day above:
    Jesus, my heavenly Bridegroom.

27. Someone's asking earnestly, "Do you love Me?"
    In His fervent longing my love to receive:
    Jesus, my heavenly Bridegroom.

28. Someone's ever waiting to hear me express
    Loving dedication and sheer faithfulness:
    Jesus, my heavenly Bridegroom.

29. Someone's pleading, "When will you give Me your love?"
    Someone's heart is grieving, "Oh, aren't I enough?"
    Jesus, my heavenly Bridegroom.

30. Someone shares His heart with me time and again,
    Giving me a glimpse of His anguish and pain:
    Jesus, my heavenly Bridegroom.

31. Someone pledged Himself to be mine evermore
    As my risen Savior and glorious Lord:
    Jesus, my heavenly Bridegroom.

29

Prayers

Called to Love Jesus

Beloved Lord Jesus,

Thank You for making and saving me that I might love You. Thank You for granting me, sinner though I am, the privilege of loving You with all my heart out of thanksgiving for Your gracious forgiveness.

Who is like You! I worship You, fairest of the sons of men. You are the most precious treasure of heaven and earth, the bright sun of my life, the joy of my heart.

Teach me to love You as You are worthy of being loved, having laid down Your life out of love for me. Nourish the spark of love in my heart with the flame of Your love, for You first loved me. Thank You that in Your love You want to give me the most precious gift of all: an intimate, fervent love, so that I might return Your love.

Thank You for this most wonderful of callings: to love You as my Lord and heavenly Bridegroom with all my heart and with all my strength. Thank You for making me completely happy and giving my life purpose.

For love of You, Lord Jesus, I want to share Your path. I don't want to leave You on Your own. Please help me to prove my love in action. I want to take up my cross and follow in Your footsteps, losing my life for Your sake by making sacrifices, learning to do without, obeying You, humbling myself—all for love of You.

Amen.

Thanksgiving for His Love

Beloved Lord Jesus,

Thank You for the privilege of loving You, because You first loved us. How blessed we are! We know that many look for love and happiness without finding it. But in You we have the fullness of joy, because You are the very essence of joy. And we may drink from the spring of Your love. Surrounded by Your love, dear Lord, we are never alone. We are privileged to do everything with You, always at Your side, living for the moment when we will be united with You above forever.

How can we ever thank You enough for revealing Yourself to us human beings as our Bridegroom, even though You are the King of Kings, Lord of all the earth, Lord of the hosts of heaven! Your choice fell upon us sinners, to whom You have drawn near in love. We thank You for pledging Yourself to us, making Yourself known to us as our Bridegroom, loving us beyond telling, always being there for us. All that is Yours is now ours, too. Who can fathom such blessings? Lord, we worship You.

Amen.

Make Me All Yours

Dear Lord Jesus,

How can I thank You for making me Your own, unworthy though I am? How can I thank You for choosing me to be Your bride?

Let me be a true bride of Yours—absorbed by Your love, giving my all for love of You. In You alone do I see all that is beautiful in heaven and on earth. In You alone do I find rest for my soul. In You alone do I have everything I need.

Make me all Yours. Make me receptive to Your love. Let me cling to You, leaning on Your strong arm. I will gladly be weak, powerless, and helpless that You, my heavenly Bridegroom, might have the joy of pouring out Your riches upon me. As Your bride I will willingly see myself for the sinner I am and take refuge in Your precious wounds, inflicted for me.

Thank You for calling me to love You as Your bride. Make me a truly loving soul, surrendered completely to You and ready for every sacrifice out of love for You. Make me a bride who shares Your innermost heart and enters the fellowship of Your sufferings.

Graciously hear my prayer.
Amen.

Take Our Hearts

Dear Lord Jesus,

Forgive us that You have to come knocking at the door of our hearts, pleading for our love. How often we have turned You away, leaving You outside in the cold. We confess with shame that we are often not ready to receive You, preferring people and things, not appreciating the treasure we have in You.

Yet You have laid down Your life for us. You love us more than words can tell. Show us what fills and stirs our hearts more than You do, keeping us from loving You first and foremost. Whatever it is, we want to bring it to You, firmly believing You will set us free for Yourself.

You long for us to love You as Your bride. You long to dwell in hearts that have thrown out their idols, making room for only You. You rejoice when we dedicate ourselves to You in this way, for then Your love can reign in us. So may we not be a source of disappointment to You any longer. Rather, let us be a source of comfort and joy.

Take our hearts, our wishes, and desires. Take all our time. We place everything in Your hands. All we want is to respond to Your love.

Amen.

Ablaze With Love

Dear Lord Jesus,

Thank You for wanting our love at all. Thank You that we can make You happy by saying, "I love You. I want to walk with You. I want to be available to You. I want to share Your concerns."

Our one prayer is that we would learn to love You more. There are still so few of Your own who love You whole-heartedly, so help us to love You above all else. Your love is like the sun! Ablaze with love, You long to set our hearts ablaze with Your fire.

We are Yours. Give us a consuming love for You that

will spur us on to do Your work in the world. Thank You that love for You is capable of turning the world upside down. Thank You that such love, fed by Your love, is greater than all else. Give us this love, we pray.

Amen.

Refresh My Soul

Dear Lord Jesus,

So long as I have You, it makes no difference if my flesh and my heart fail. I will not be afraid, for You are with me, Jesus, my Bridegroom.

And though an army besiege me, You will be my comfort and my support. You are strong and mighty. You have conquered hell. Every enemy must bow before You. You are Lord—Lord over everything that oppresses me. You made heaven and earth.

As my Beloved You are all this and far more. So why should I fear? As I lean upon You, my soul is refreshed.

Thank You that with this encouragement I can go through times of spiritual dryness and overcome attacks of the Evil One, secure in the knowledge that I am one with You. Nothing is stronger than the fellowship of love. Through Your presence You transform the desert into a garden and refresh my soul, enabling me to share with others the comfort of Your love when they are going through a desert experience. Thank You, dear Lord.

Amen.

Love Stronger Than Death

Dear Lord Jesus,

Your love is stronger than death. Please fill us with Your

love so that we do not deny You in the hour of testing.

Help us to practice by making the small sacrifices that daily life presents so that, should we be called to do so, we can pay the ultimate sacrifice in the hour of trial. Give us the strength to love You above all else, regardless of any pain. You know how we dread suffering of body and soul. You know our fear that we may waver if faced with a choice between relief and proving our allegiance to You, possibly with our lives.

Once again we ask You: Fill us with the mighty stream of Your love so that in our hour of trial You will not be disappointed in us but can say gladly and with thanksgiving, "How sweet is Your love, My sister, My bride!"

Amen.

I Want Jesus, Only Jesus

Lord Jesus,
Make me strong, courageous, and steadfast,
afire with love for You,
wholly dedicated,
granite-like with determination,
having but one aim:
I want Jesus, only Jesus.
I will not seek relief or ease
or the comfort of seeing and feeling.
All I want, dear Lord,
is by faith to embrace You
and to love You in times of testing
when all is dark.

Amen.
Mother Martyria

Nothing Shall Be Dearer to Me

Nothing shall be dearer to me than You, Lord.
Nothing shall absorb me apart from You, Lord.
Nothing shall cause me to lament but Your pain.
Nothing shall inflame my heart but You alone.
Nothing shall grieve me but Your grief over sin.
Mind and soul shall be centered on You alone:
Every thought, emotion, desire, intention.
All I want is You—Jesus, Jesus, Jesus.

Amen.

With You, Lord Jesus

With You, Lord Jesus, I can face
The fears, the insults and disgrace
In times of persecution.
When You are there, my soul will sing,
And suffering will lose its sting.
I'm resting on Your bosom.

With You I live from day to day
And when my heart is torn with pain,
Your love has healing power.
A single ray of love divine
Brings heaven down, dispels the night,
Transcending scenes of horror.

With You beside me I will tread
Secure in time of war and death
And widespread devastation.
Amid the terrors I may rest,
A little child by love caressed
And trusting in Your leading.

With You, all suffering turns to gain,
A blessing comes from every pain,
A harvest reaped from sorrow.
The crown of life, the wedding feast,
Celestial joys and endless peace
Await the bride of Jesus.

We Come Adoring

We come adoring, reverently gazing
Upon the holy Lamb of God,
Longing to honor Jesus our Savior,
Lowliness choosing for His sake.

We come adoring, bowing in meekness,
Grieving to see You mocked and scorned,
Our voices raising, Your glories praising:
Fairest of all, Lord Jesus Christ.

We kneel, lamenting, our sins confessing,
Every affront to Love divine.
By our transgressing we've caused You anguish,
Broken Your loving heart again.

Seeing Your anguish, holy Redeemer,
Kindles a longing deep within:
Oh, to be sharing Your pain and suffering,
Bearing our cross for love of You!

One day You'll come, establish Your kingdom,
Amid rejoicing and acclaim.
But now we're mourning, with our Lord weeping
Over the malice, the hurtful shame.

O None Can Be Loved As Is Jesus

O none can be loved as is Jesus.
None like Him is found anywhere.
'Tis He whom I love, whom I live for,
For no one with Him can compare.

So all that I have I will give Him,
I'll sacrifice all I hold dear.
My whole life to Jesus belonging,
My heart seeks my Lord to revere.

I follow now close in His footsteps
The path that He trod here below.
I only desire what He gives me,
And only His way I will go.

My heart is at peace and so joyful,
For all I desire He supplies.
I look now for nothing but Jesus,
Who all of my hopes satisfies.

Who Makes As Happy, Lord Jesus, As You?

Who makes as happy, Lord Jesus, as You?
Therefore my heart rejoices in You,
Jesus, O Joy eternal!

Jesus, my wellspring of joy ever new,
Heaven's great joy to us comes through You,
Jesus, O Joy eternal!

Jesus, my joy-spring, flow into my heart,
Bringing me joy, make sorrow depart,
Jesus, O Joy eternal!

You create gladness when hearts let You in,
For You cleanse guilt and blot out all sin,
Jesus, O Joy eternal!

Kingdom of heaven shall truly begin
Where sinners are repenting of sin,
Jesus, O Joy eternal!

Jesus, my Savior, my God and my King,
You fill my heart with praises to sing,
Jesus, O Joy eternal!

Jesus, my joy-spring so deep and so broad,
Joy on this earth You've richly outpoured,
But oh the joy when we see You!

I Sing Aloud, Who Can With You Compare?

I sing aloud, who can with You compare
Here on the earth, in heaven, or anywhere.
No, none with You, Lord Jesus, can compare,
And none Your splendid glory ever share.
Who is like You?

I sing aloud, I sing of One alone,
His is the name that ever in me sounds.
O Jesus, Jesus, I am all Your own.
I am Your bride, my praise for You abounds,
To give You joy.

I sing aloud, Your majesty I praise,
For I am Yours—what joy to be Your bride,
Who knows Your heart and all Your loving ways,
And shares Your joy and sorrow at Your side
With pride and love!

No Words Can Worthily Express

No words can worthily express
The majesty and loveliness
Of my dear Lord and Savior.
Out of You shines God's glorious light,
His perfect image, radiant, bright,
Jesus, O matchless Sovereign.

Angelic choirs before You fall,
Offering praise in humble awe,
Glorious, gracious Jesus.
Jubilant songs resound at the throne,
Honoring God's beloved Son,
Blessed, most holy Jesus.

What majesty and radiance
Shines from my Jesus' countenance
In all the heavenly regions!
The saints of God reflect this light,
For the Lamb's nature in their lives
Shines forth, God glorifying.

O Lamb enthroned in heaven above,
King of the ages, Son of God,
Fairest, glorious Jesus.
I humbly worship and adore,
Filled with amazement, wondering awe
To be a bride of Jesus.

All Praise to the Lamb of God

All praise to the Lamb of God,
Bridegroom and glorious Lord,
Splendid in majesty.
The church triumphant sings,
Making all heaven ring
With joyous strains of praise.

Not one voice silent now,
All low in worship bow,
Praising our God enthroned.
With joy each one casts down
Before the Lord his crown,
Acclaiming Him as King.

Joy bursts from every heart,
Praising the Lamb of God
Enthroned in highest heaven.
Radiant His countenance,
Inspiring reverence
In heaven for evermore.

O Countenance

O countenance of beauty and of holiness,
O countenance endowed with God's eternal peace,
O countenance of Him, our matchless Sovereign,
O countenance more dazzling than the brightest sun,
How glorious, how winsome, how lovely You are!

In Your features the holiness of the Godhead
can be seen, so majestic and exalted.

From You sprang the glories of creation,
upon which Your radiant countenance ever shines.
All that is noble and lovely is to be found in You.
And in Your gracious, loving countenance,
love itself is reflected.

Lord, enthroned in majesty
high above the cherubim,
high above the hosts of heaven,
high above all stars and worlds,
robed in power and splendor,
how awesome is Your countenance.
Earth and sky will flee at Your presence,
the glories of this world fade into nothingness.
O perfect image of the invisible God,
what bliss to worship You for evermore,
lost in wonder, praise, and awe!

One sight alone will enrapture my heart in eternity,
one theme alone inspire me with unceasing songs of praise:
Your countenance, O fairest of the sons of men,
Majesty Divine,
before whom all heaven prostrate falls,
hushed in reverence.

Your countenance!
How sweetly sounds the music of the harps!
Throughout the heavens worshiping angels
sing their anthems in praise of this countenance,
so holy, so splendid, so divinely fair,
bathing heaven in its glorious light.

The vision of Your countenance so infinitely loving
brings healing to the world.
It shines with wondrous radiance, brighter than
a myriad suns.
It loves and heals, refreshes and restores,
drawing erring children home to their Lord.

Exalted in beauty,
exalted in glory,
exalted in majesty,
Your countenance holds me captive.
My heart is forever Yours.

30
Testimonies from Kanaan

All for Christ

Toward the end of a summer vacation at Kanaan, one question weighed upon my mind: How could I best serve my Lord for the rest of my life? Soon I was due to graduate from university. I was set on continuing my studies and was aiming for a doctorate in physics or chemistry. Plans concerning all this were whirling around in my head, because I had already been given a wonderful opportunity to do some research. Physics was my life and my love—almost everything I ever thought about had to do with it.

In the previous year, Jesus, in His love, had released me from an agnostic way of thinking. Then, while studying the Scriptures during my summer vacation at Kanaan, I became aware of the Lord grieving because we do not love Him enough. I was deeply convicted. All sorts of questions flooded my mind: How could I give Him the love He so much longs for? Should I volunteer to assist in the work of my church? Or should I perhaps begin some sort of ministry among students? Or, again, should I give up my scientific studies and become a minister? Should I get married—or should I remain single in order to be more available for Him? Would my family and friends approve of such a course of action? Would they even understand? In brief, how did the Lord want me to serve Him?

With all this on my mind, I asked advice while still at Kanaan. The answer was quite simple: "Seek *Jesus*, Jesus alone. He will show you the next step, and the one after that, if you seek *Him* alone. Spend no more time going over the various options—just spend time with Him." It was suggested that I be still before the Lord and make this a matter of serious prayer.

When I returned to America at the end of that summer, I was still without any definite leading. But I continued to pray, in the assurance that God answers prayer. As time passed, some doors closed and others opened. Then, quite suddenly, the Lord gave me deep repentance, showing me how I had continually neglected Him by lavishing my love and time on people and things rather than on Him.

My eyes were opened, and instantly everything was clear. Now I knew what the Lord was asking of me. Now, in keeping with His Word, I wanted to give up everything for Him—even my family and home, my country, and everything that went with it. Now I did not find it difficult at all, because He was worth it. Now He was the joy of my life, my first and foremost love. Physics just does not begin to compare with Jesus! He is my heavenly Bridegroom, the source of all love and joy, not only for this life but for all eternity.

I wanted to leap and sing out of love for Jesus. I was so

happy that He was calling me to dedicate my whole life to Him. What tremendous love! Later, at my investiture as a Canaan Franciscan Brother, the Lord in His tender love confirmed my vocation with the Scripture, "As the bridegroom rejoices over the bride, so shall your God rejoice over you" (Isaiah 62:5).

—Brother Sylvestro

———————

"The sun has scorched me."
Song of Songs 1:6

After serving abroad for several years, I welcomed the chance to return from the "desert" to Kanaan, our headquarters in Germany. In the desert I had been deprived of many of the blessings of fellowship, and so I looked forward to a spiritual abundance. Yet in spite of the abundance I felt cold and unresponsive. I could not understand what was happening. I grew sad and began to pity myself. Then gradually I came to realize that there was a barrier blocking the way to Jesus' heart. What had happened?

When I first left Kanaan, I found it hard. To obey God's call had been a major sacrifice. However, with the passage of time, this changed, though unnoticed by me. Instead of involving sacrifice, my work became an increasing source of satisfaction; unconsciously, as I grew satisfied and sure of myself, my service became more self-centered than Christ-centered. Spiritually I was stagnating, and consequently my service for Jesus lost its spiritual cutting edge.

Then I realized that Jesus' words applied to me: "But this is what I have against you: you do not love me now as you did at first. Think how far you have fallen! Turn from your sins and do what you did at first" (Revelation 2:4–5 TEV). The eye-salve (Revelation 3:18) bringing me this recognition was at first very painful; but as soon as I had fully accepted Jesus' verdict and had humbled myself before Him, the barrier between us fell. I began to weep and rejoice and worship Him all at the same time. A new love was born. His presence was almost tangible. Words fail me when I try to describe it.

Again, repentance had been the gateway to a new bridal love for Jesus. . . . Time and again it has been my experience that repentance enables me to discover more deeply what I am like and, most wonderful of all, what He is like, who He is, and how much He is to be loved.

—Sister Cäcilie

"I sought him."
Song of Songs 3:2

During the winter of 1959 I spent many pleasurable hours playing the church organ in Brevik, Norway. It was wonderful to be abroad for the first time, and it was marvelous to be an organist, even though my main purpose was to learn how to keep house! I loved music more than anything else and had just passed my examinations in sacred music. It was a happy, carefree time, which I enjoyed thoroughly. To be sure, I loved Jesus, having belonged to Him since childhood, but my love had not led to a dedicated Christian life.

I cannot really say how it happened, but one evening, as I finished practicing on the organ, I had an irresistible urge to dedicate my life completely to Jesus, to surrender everything to Him. Although I was actually on my way out, I went back into the empty church and sang:

> Lord, my Shepherd, Fount of all joys,
> You are mine, I am Yours.
> None can ever part us.
>   —Paul Gerhardt (1607–1676)

With the uncanny conviction that my prayer was already answered, I left for the small nearby village where I was living.

That same evening, just two hours later, I was on my way to a friend's house. The sky glowed a strange red. A child ran by, shouting in Norwegian, "The church is burning!" Though not comprehending, I ran the rest of the way up the hill, from where I saw Brevik Church in a sea of flames. (I learned later that a defect in the heating system had caused the fire.) All I remember is falling down on my knees in the deep snow, convicted by the holiness of God, and praying for His mercy. It was not only the shock of seeing the house of God on fire, but the realization that all my organ music, collected over the years, and all my other possessions, from singing manuals to a metronome, were going up in smoke before my very eyes.

Jesus knew my divided heart, and, in a flash, He showed me the truth about myself. I had been living in pious deception. But, in that moment, I was freed from my preoccupation with music. Now I understood that I could not have Jesus as the dearest of all unless I gave up my dearest and best. Since then I have discovered what a wonderful exchange that is. How little is the worth of what we forsake compared with the untold riches of what we gain!

—Sister Justina

"He restores my soul."
Psalm 23:3

On the day of my bridal dedication as a Sister of Mary, I received a sprig of mimosa with a card saying, "May you love Jesus, your heavenly Bridegroom, with a love as tender and sensitive as the mimosa."

Many years later I accompanied Mother Basilea to the Sinai Peninsula. Here the Lord had made an eternal covenant of love with His people. A pain shot through my heart: Although Jesus had made a covenant with me on the day of my bridal dedication, how little had I responded to His love. That same day, at Mount Sinai, a tourist from another country working on a photographic assignment brought me a sprig of mimosa. He just wanted to share his joy at having found such a flower at the Sinai Massif with its scant vegetation. Instantly, I recognized the sign and the One who had really given me the flower.

A few years later, on the anniversary of my bridal dedication, I was in Scandinavia. Constant demands were made upon me, and I was greatly in need of spiritual refreshment. I wondered, *Dear Lord Jesus, have I grieved You in some way, making You withdraw Your presence?* Worn out, I returned to my hotel, only to sigh wearily upon learning that someone wanted to see me. But this lady, whom I did not know, merely wanted to give me some flowers—mimosa! His love forgets nothing.

—Sister Benedicta

―――――

"Look and see if there is any sorrow like my sorrow."
Lamentations 1:12

Jesus has a unique way of winning our love, though not as we might expect. He does not promise us only good things, a life free from hardship. Rather, His most compelling attraction, that which inspires a soul to love Him with bridal love, lies in His Passion.

Among us there is a young sister from Arizona. What brought her to Kanaan? Her father and brother are pilots. She herself had planned to become a teacher. Jesus was only a vague concept to her, but that was to change. It was Holy Week. On the night of Maundy Thursday–Good Friday, she meditated with our sisters in Phoenix on the Passion of Christ and worshiped Him as the Man of Sorrows. As she prayed, *How can I thank You for what You suffered to save me?* she knew she could thank Him only by dedicating her whole life to Him.

The Garden of Jesus' Sufferings, at Kanaan, testifies to all that He suffered for love of us. Many visitors have met with the Lord in this garden. They have wept tears of repentance, accepted their sufferings, heard the call of God, and experienced the rekindling of their love for Jesus.

Many guests have told us that the most decisive and precious hours of their stay at Kanaan were spent in the Garden of Jesus' Sufferings.

A single hour there transformed the life of a young Scandinavian. The sculpture depicting Jesus despised, forsaken, and crowned with thorns made an indelible impression upon her. At that she gave up everything—her home, her career prospects, her desire for marriage and a family, in order to serve Jesus in lowliness and obedience, and that in a country which had committed grievous crimes against her own.

A young man whom it seemed counseling could not help any further was in the Garden of Jesus' Sufferings. Challenged by this visible reminder of how much Jesus suffered for him, he found his way from rebellion to commitment.

At one point in the history of our sisterhood, an especially severe wave of defamatory attacks descended upon our mothers. As spiritual daughters we were understandably saddened, and one of us finally put our feelings into words: "There's no one to defend you." Mother Basilea's brief but matter-of-fact reply was more effective than a dozen sermons: "Have you forgotten the scene from the Prayer Garden showing Jesus standing trial all by Himself? Why do you think it is there?"

—Sister Ruth

———

"Sing aloud . . . O daughter of Jerusalem."
Zephaniah 3:14

When invited to give a talk about our sisterhood or when speaking with visiting groups, we are invariably asked what we actually do! While we are happy to respond to this question, we always find that some points are hard to explain to those unfamiliar with Kanaan. The purpose of some of our ministries is not immediately obvious, since they cannot be measured against the yardstick of human usefulness. The ministry on the Mount of Olives in Jerusalem falls into this category.

As Mother Basilea once wrote, "Oh, if only songs of love and thanksgiving would fill Jerusalem and the tongues of those who love the Lord never fall silent! The Via Dolorosa, for instance, is filled with noise, dirt, and commercialism. How sad it is to hear the muezzins cry out day and night from the minarets to remind the faithful of their prayer duties! Who will dedicate his life so that Jesus may receive love and adoration here? Who will help challenge others to make some sacrifice in order to go on pilgrimage to the Holy Land, there to worship Jesus and to sing His praises in a world largely ignoring Him?"

"Sing wherever you go," were Mother Basilea's parting words as she left the three of us to begin a ministry on the Mount of Olives, a new little branch wonderfully prepared by God for us. And sing we did—so much so that people said we must come from a singing order! Though privileged to see the ministry among the poor, as well as that among tourists and pilgrims, expand during our time in Jerusalem, we have never lost sight of the basic reason for this Holy Land ministry: to glorify Jesus in song.

—The sisters on the Mount of Olives

————

"Why this waste?"
Matthew 26:8

In Switzerland's Bernese Oberland, we were led to build two praise chapels to the glory of God. Each has its own story to tell. For example, when building the first one, we were in a very difficult financial position, having just completed the Herald Chapel at Kanaan with its seating capacity of one thousand. To begin with, the whole idea failed in many quarters to find favor. There was little understanding even among our friends. The question persisted as to why more financial outlay was necessary. Why another chapel—and why in Switzerland?

Building costs were much exaggerated by rumor. One Swiss woman finally took all her questions to her minister. Who would benefit from such a building? What useful purpose would it serve? Surely the money could have been better invested. Later she shared with us her minister's reply: "Well, a lot is being done for people. But who is ready to do something for God and for His glory? Isn't there a time to give to Him?" This is the way first love, bridal love, thinks.

Over the years many have visited both praise chapels. Praise and prayer, counseling and encouragement, are all part of the ministry of these chapels—built for His glory, now used by Him to refresh many.

—Sister Myrrhia

"A garden enclosed is my sister."
Song of Songs 4:12 NKJV

The verse from the Psalms that prophetically utters the lament of our suffering Lord—"I looked . . . for comforters"

(Psalm 69:20)—pierced my heart as a young Sister of Mary. But who can comfort Jesus?—Only someone who cares deeply about Him, His agony and suffering, and who shares His present-day anguish over a world which He loves but which largely rejects Him; only someone who can forget his own suffering. I truly longed to be a comforter of Jesus, refreshing Him and bringing Him joy. Time and again I wrote in my diary a prayer echoing the longing of my heart. . . . How different, though, my life in reality!

In our sisterhood it is customary for a younger sister not only to go to our mothers for spiritual counseling, but also to have the opportunity of sharing with one of the more mature sisters assigned to her for that purpose. And so it was perfectly normal that I made frequent use of this opportunity during a particular time of spiritual dryness. Yet I often sensed that Jesus wanted me to forgo for once the comfort of having someone sympathize with me when I felt inwardly dry. I knew He wanted me to make this sacrifice freely, for His sake. But usually I was too weak.

Once when I was feeling discouraged because I seemed to fail every day, I wanted to speak with the sister assigned to me. However, at that time she was very busy, having many responsibilities. In my self-centered way I reacted hypersensitively, feeling that she was not as kind and sympathetic as usual. Soon afterward the Spirit of God opened my eyes and showed me how anxious I was to receive understanding, love, and attention. I could only weep in repentance for having been so inconsiderate toward this sister. But more importantly, I now grieved that in my self-absorption I had so often forgotten Jesus. In my longing to receive comfort for myself, I had failed to become a comforter for Him.

Now I had but a single thought: *Spend more time in prayer. Come to Him and tell Him everything.* And I knew exactly what I had to do: Admit my failings to my sisters whenever necessary, but not to go looking for sympathy by wallowing in self-pity about my particular weaknesses of character. If something continued to get me down, I should bring it to Him alone.

The Lord granted me this experience just ten days before Christmas. And that Christmas I knew the grace of God more than ever. I was blessed by the sense of His presence. I could spend hours in prayer alone with Him, desiring nothing else.

—Sister Salome

———

"He cared for him."
Deuteronomy 32:10

Pleasant surprises are very welcome, but unpleasant surprises are just the reverse—and the less they are expected, the bigger the shock and the more they hurt. Over the years we have noticed in our Bible readings how gently Jesus prepared His disciples for the time of His sufferings so that they might not be quite so devastated when the time came.

One day as I was walking along, my mind busy with ordinary things, it seemed as though someone were knocking gently on the door of my heart. Suddenly I knew, *Something very difficult is going to happen. Everything will depend on how you take it.*

Later that same day, something I had forgotten for years came back to mind and hit me where I was most vulnerable. Now I saw the incident from a different perspective and felt very guilty. I was tempted to despair, because the situation seemed hopelessly beyond me. Then I remembered what the Lord had impressed upon my heart only hours earlier: *Everything will depend on how you take it.* With this came such assurance! And I knew that having warned and prepared me so lovingly, my Lord would also deal with my guilt and cancel the effects of my wrongdoing. I need not despair.

—Sister Benedicta

––––––––––

"I have this against you."
Revelation 2:4

At an early age I knew something of first love for Jesus. For love of Him I had joyfully sacrificed everything: parents and friends, home and all that went with it. I followed Him and devoted my life to serving Him. I knew both the joy of Jesus knocking at the door of my heart and the joy of letting Him in. . . . But we can still be self-seeking, even when we seem to have given up everything to follow Jesus. How often our desire is for spiritual enjoyment!

One day I was devastated to discover that this was true of me. I wanted the blessings of bridal love but not Jesus Himself, who says, "If anyone loves me, he will obey my teaching" (John 14:23 NIV). Although God had spoken to me through James 4:10, "Humble yourselves before the Lord," I was unwilling. Because all sense of Jesus' love was gone, I grumbled and complained, even thinking like the servant in the parable that God was a harsh master, making unfair demands (Matthew 25:24). This is what I thought of God, and this is what I experienced. My work was no longer under His blessing. I was restless and could not concentrate. Even in prayer my rebellious thoughts pursued me.

For a long time I was very unhappy. Then one night I dreamed that I was to become a bride of Jesus again. I was shocked to realize that I was no longer a bride. But our Bible reading that day confirmed it: "I have this against you, that you have abandoned the love you had at first" (Revelation 2:4). At last I humbled myself beneath the hand of God, willing to be convicted by His Word. And what happened? Revelation 3:20 gives the answer: "If any one hears my voice and opens the door, I will come in to him and eat with him, and he with me."

At that time I was having some quiet days, and there were moments when Jesus knocked at the door of my heart—far more than in earlier years, when I had first met Him as my heavenly Bridegroom. Now nothing else mattered—reading, walking, eating, or sleeping. The hours sped by, for Jesus was there.

—Sister Eusebia

———

Alone With the Lord

Many of the guests attending our retreats have commented that the best day is the Quiet Day. Upon opening their door in the morning, they are surprised to find a slip of paper bearing the words, "I am waiting for you." For many it was a revelation that Jesus is more eager for an encounter with us than we are for an encounter with Him.

An incident from the early years of the sisterhood illustrates the fact that Jesus longs to have fellowship with us. When the first stage of our building project was finished, we lived together in close quarters in the Motherhouse, some of us sleeping in bunk beds. The number of occupants in a room was based on the available space rather than on the need for quiet. It certainly helped us to learn how to get along with one another! But there was a growing desire for a prayer closet (Matthew 6:6). Our mothers prayed about this and received the assurance that Jesus Himself would provide. There would be an extension to the Motherhouse containing only small single rooms—our prayer closets.

We could not help feeling awed when the bills for this second stage of our building project were paid with relative ease. How often our faith had been tested to its limits when we were building! But this time His blessing was very obvious. We had never experienced anything like it. This extension with its small single rooms must really have been pleasing to the Lord.

We will never forget the day we moved in. We walked through the house singing songs of worship. In each room Mother Basilea had placed in the prayer corner the printed message, "I am waiting for you." Yes, He really is waiting!

This is why the first guest house to be built at Kanaan contains nearly all single rooms. And this is also why it became customary for every guest to receive the words, "I am waiting for you" at the beginning of a Quiet Day.

—Sister Eulalia

The Divine Perspective

While preparations were underway for Mother Basilea's trip to India, a great deal of literature about that country came into our hands. We were overwhelmed by the human misery conveyed in word and picture. Then came the first lengthy report from India, written by the sister accompanying Mother Basilea. This added a fresh dimension to our understanding as well as bringing an unexpected challenge.

Our sister had written, "At a religious festival here in India, a decorated cow was led through the streets to a rapturous welcome from thousands of spectators. Mother Basilea was deeply grieved that a mere animal should receive such adulation, compared to the lack of enthusiasm so often evident among those professing to love Jesus. For religious reasons people are virtually starving themselves so that the sacred cow may live. How does our commitment to Jesus measure up?"

All further reports from India continued to stress the importance of seeing things from the divine perspective. Love for Jesus enables us to see everything through the eyes and heart of the Beloved. And then our view becomes both horizontal and vertical.

—Sister Rebekka

A Question of Love

Apart from the fact that I sought to love Jesus and, for His sake, had given up everything that made life worth living for me—my family, my freedom, my career—I knew nothing when I entered the Sisterhood of Mary.

As I began to realize how much this way of life was costing me, my initial enthusiasm began to wane. Gradually I ceased to fight the good fight and gave up. One day it all seemed to be over. But not for Jesus! "Don't you love Jesus?" was the question someone who did love Him asked me lovingly. It pierced my heart.

"Don't you love Jesus?" Stirred by this question, I began a new life. As I repeated this question to myself, all the things that had previously been burdensome suddenly became easy. I found myself welcoming that which had gone against the grain. I grew happier and happier. And now, whenever anything threatens to overwhelm me, the same question comes to mind: "Don't you love Jesus?" And when I reply, "Yes, Jesus, I do love You," then His words come true: "My yoke is easy, and my burden is light" (Matthew 11:30).

—Sister Claudia

An Undivided Heart

There was a certain time of testing in my life that I found difficult to accept. Not until some years later could I say with hindsight, "What a blessing that Jesus watches us closely to ensure that we love Him with single-minded devotion." For a while I had a task at Kanaan that gave me much satisfaction. I was completely taken up with it. I loved my work! It gave me organizational responsibilities and allowed me scope for creativity. Then, it so happened that I was transferred to another area of work. Jesus seemed to be saying no to what I had done. My initial reaction was disappointment. I thought He no longer loved me and had forgotten me.

The truth was exactly the opposite. And God graciously brought His light to my darkness. Then, filled with contrition and shame, I had to admit, "I have forgotten You. I have not loved You above all else. Rather I have loved my work. I have loved myself. But You in Your love have reached out to me with Your chastening hand. You took me at my word when I said I wanted to love You above all else."

The truth sank in. Weeping over my sin, I found my way back to the One who wouldn't accept a divided heart from me. Still in tears, I was gripped with a joyous sense of wonder: *Why me? How did I come to receive such love? I will never begin to understand that You should love a sinner like me so dearly and that I may love You in return.*

—Sister Gabriele

———

"My beloved had turned and gone."
Song of Songs 5:6

If only we could learn to praise the Lord whenever He allows us to suffer in some way when we are in danger of becoming overattached to people and work instead of giving Him our love! How He must love us if He would chasten us, even allow us to suffer, rather than see our love diminished in any way. Happy are those who are loved so dearly that even the smallest things can affect such a special relationship. This is why what is allowed to others is not necessarily permissible for them.

A holiday in the quiet of the countryside—how I had been looking forward to going away! This was to be a time of prayer and preparation for an important new chapter in my life. But the joy of anticipation was soon overtaken by the disappointment of reality. The quiet for which I had yearned proved empty, and my prayers seemed to rebound from the ceiling. The Bible no longer spoke to me. I did not understand what God was doing. Was I not here just to listen to Him?

A verse from Micah 7 was my answer: "I will bear the indignation of the Lord because I have sinned against him" (v. 9). I recalled the past weeks. I had been very busy. My work had so engrossed me that I was already thinking about it during my morning quiet time. I hardly thought of Jesus all day. Any spare time I had was spent with a loved one who was visiting me.

Had not Jesus in His great love commanded us to abide in Him? How I must have grieved Him. Love scorned is one of life's most painful experiences—yet this was how I had treated Jesus. Deeply dismayed, I began to grasp more fully the wonder of His love. He wants to have us close to Him throughout the day. But if I do not want to be with Him, then He cannot be with me. How holy is His claim on our love. Amazingly, as I accepted the disappointment of His withdrawing the sense of His presence, I had a deep inner peace and the assurance that He loved me. So out of that painful experience came blessing.

—Sister Dolores

————

"It was granted her to be clothed with fine linen."
Revelation 19:8

It must be thirty years ago now that I was leafing through a fashion magazine. I turned page after page, looking for the wedding dress I thought I would like to wear someday. At last I found one that was exactly my taste—simple in design, with long, flowing lines. It was just perfect! This was the dress in which I would greet my bridegroom on our wedding day. I dreamed of a strong, deep love, of a mutual giving and receiving, of being completely at one in our Christian faith. I met many fine people who enriched my life, but I did not find what I was looking for. In my longing for satisfaction I concentrated on a few friendships, but deep down inside I was lonely. Years later, while tidying up one day, I found that page from the fashion magazine. The wedding dress I had chosen had turned yellow with the passage of time. Eventually I threw the clipping away. It did not seem likely that the kind of love I was still seeking really did exist—or did it?

Then I visited Ranft, the valley in Switzerland where Nicholas von der Flüe had lived a sacrificial life of prayer, becoming a recluse for love of his Lord. Though five hundred years had passed, the whole atmosphere of his hermitage breathed the spirit of dedication and prayer. There in the quiet the Lord began to remind me of His love, which was still waiting for me.

I had known Jesus since my youth, and He had been faithful to me over the years, even when I had neglected Him and pursued my own interests.

I cannot remember much about leaving Ranft Valley. All I knew was that I could no longer avoid His claim upon me for undivided love. It meant parting with my dearest and best in order to experience more fully the love of Him who had waited so long in vain for me. I felt a strong inner compulsion to follow Him wherever He led. He led me into the Sisterhood of Mary.

To begin with, Jesus did not meet with me as the heavenly Bridegroom. I could not approach Him as I was then—so sure of myself and so "pious." The old rags serving to cover my spiritual nakedness, my weak points, had to go. Then when I faced up to what I was really like, when I could find nothing good in myself, when I could only cry to the Lord for mercy because of my sin, He came to me, He whom I could now love so intimately. As I came to see how greatly He had suffered for my sake, He drew me to Himself.

Today if anyone were to ask me, "Is there really love such as you used to dream of—strong and deep, satisfying you completely?" my whole being would rejoice in reply: "Yes, there is such a love! And it is a thousand times more beautiful than the love I had yearned for! This love cannot be compared with human love. This is a tender, selfless, sympathetic love, a love that refreshes and comforts. This love never disappoints. It is stronger than death. It draws me up to heaven and is leading me to the marriage supper—the wedding—of the Lamb."

Wedding? Once again I recalled the yellowing page with my

dream wedding dress. I no longer need that dress. For this wedding, for the marriage supper of the Lamb, I do not have to prepare my wedding dress. I believe that an even more beautiful one will have been prepared for me—one woven out of much suffering and washed in the blood of the Lamb. This dress will never turn yellow, not through all eternity! Its purity will forever reveal the infinite love of Jesus.

—Sister Nicola

Other literature by Basilea Schlink

Behold His Love   hardback   216 pages
As I walked in spirit with Jesus from Gethsemane to Calvary, I saw myself in all
the major players of the Passion. I felt with Him the pain. I saw into His heart.
And I was awed by the love that nothing, literally nothing, could kill.   UK

Building a Wall of Prayer An intercessor's handbook   96 pages
When the future of a nation is in the balance, when politics, economics and ethics
fail, it is the intercessors who can make a difference.

I Found the Key to the Heart of God   416 pages
Autobiography
3600 metres high up in the Himalayas a copy of Mother Basilea Schlink's autobiogaphy
reached me and my colleagues in a dark hour. Initially we were regarded with favour
by the authorities and our service was under God's blessing. Then all of a sudden we
found ourselves having to give up our work and leave the country. What had happened
to all the promises God had given us? This book was the answer in that heart-searching
time.   Switzerland

More Precious Than Gold   Daily readings, hardback   416 pages
I am looking forward to walking my way through this year and years to come
with this as my guide.   USA

Realities of Faith   144 pages
Experiences of answered prayer at Kanaan. This is a book for a prayer group,
for it is so faith-inspiring. It makes wonderful reading for family devotions. And
children will love the stories.   USA

Repentance – The Joy-Filled Life   80 pages
Excerpt: Repentance – the gateway to heaven! Repentance – the way home to the
Father's heart. For what is repentance but the tailwind driving us into the open arms
of the Father? A foretaste of heaven. A gift of the Holy Spirit. In answer to prayer
the Holy Spirit falls afresh on us, breaking our hard and self-righteous hearts – only
for God our Father and Maker to take those broken pieces into His hands and form
a new vessel to His glory.

Ruled by the Spirit   130 pages

I was a Muslim army officer in Pakistan when Jesus appeared to me in a dazzling light, as He did to Saul on the road to Damascus. "Ruled by the Spirit" was the first Christian book I read upon my arrival in Australia; and although it was twenty years ago, I have never forgotten it.   Pastor, Australia

Shine Light into my Darkness: 98 pages

Winning the War Against Despondency

hardback, full colour

Mother Basilea has written a most useful book which contains much biblical truth and insight and, best of all, ways of applying this in our lives. Some-one who imbibes and applies the truth and insight contained in this book should experience a good change in their life from despondency to joy!

Christian counsellor, Scotland

The Royal Priesthood   48 pages

Excerpt: "Human souls are like jewels. Cherished and precious in God's sight, they are to be carried prayerfully by the priest into the sanctuary, into the presence of God. There, in the light of God, they begin to shine, just as a jewel sparkles when placed in the light."

Sown in Weakness, Raised in Glory   168 pages

From the spiritual legacy of Mother Basilea Schlink

hard cover, full colour throughout

As I face the testings of the end times, this book has become one of my spiritual guides. Mother Basilea's testimony and her loving dedication to the Lord Jesus through trials and suffering encourages me greatly.   USA

The Unseen World of Angels and Demons   136 pages

In a country non-accessable to missionaries, an indigenous Christian who received a copy in the local language is now travelling from village to village and has been greatly used by God.   East Asia

Patmos – When the Heavens Opened   128 pages

The Book of Revelation comes alive

Have already read it 5 times myself. My favourite chapter is "The 144,000 on Mount Zion". Whenever I feel crushed, I read that description and instantly I'm lifted into Heavenly Regions; new strength is given me and I can again begin to "run the race" with a fresh picture of my goal before my eyes.   USA